Praise

'This book offers a refreshing and relatable approach to entrepreneurship.'
— **Linda Carmichael,** consultant,
  the Proctor Gallagher Institute

'If you truly want to unlock the entrepreneur within, this is the book for you. It is full of practical advice from Melanie, who has grown her own business.'
— **Alison Matthews,** founder,
  VirtuAli Admin Solutions

'This book has been a lifesaver for me. It is a fantastic business companion, full of inspiring practical and professional advice.'
— **Linda Hyde,** interior designer,
  Sunburst Interior Design

UNLOCK THE **ENTREPRENEUR** WITHIN

Dream big.
Work smart.
Make it happen.

Melanie Coey

Rethink

First published in Great Britain in 2022
by Rethink Press (www.rethinkpress.com)

© Copyright Melanie Coey

All rights reserved. No part of this publication may be reproduced, stored in or introduced into a retrieval system, or transmitted, in any form, or by any means (electronic, mechanical, photocopying, recording or otherwise) without the prior written permission of the publisher.

The right of Melanie Coey to be identified as the author of this work has been asserted by her in accordance with the Copyright, Designs and Patents Act 1988.

This book is sold subject to the condition that it shall not, by way of trade or otherwise, be lent, resold, hired out, or otherwise circulated without the publisher's prior consent in any form of binding or cover other than that in which it is published and without a similar condition including this condition being imposed on the subsequent purchaser.

Cover image © Shutterstock | Oleh Svetiukha and Fagreia

*This book is dedicated to my amazing children,
my heroes Saul and Kai Coey. They are the reason
I strive to achieve my goals every single day.*

Contents

Foreword	1
Introduction	5
PART ONE Where to Begin	11
1 **Start**	13
Feeling stuck and overwhelmed	14
How to avoid the business plateau	19
Believe in yourself	24
Fear of growth	28
Fear of failure	32
Roadmap to success	35
Summary	40
2 **Question**	41
What is your why?	42
How do you grow?	46

Are you confident at making decisions?	49
Who can you ask for help?	51
How big are your goals?	56
Summary	60

PART TWO Changing Your Mindset — 63

3 Understand Yourself — 65

Understand your passion	66
Understand your vulnerability	69
Understand why you should compete only with yourself	73
Understand how to build resilience	77
Understand why you should act on your goals	82
Summary	84

4 Align — 87

Align with gratitude	88
Align your thoughts	92
Align with your intuition	95
Align your self-esteem and confidence	99
Summary	105

5 Results — 107

Service	108
Work smarter, not harder	111

Focus	113
Growth mindset	117
Abundance	119
Summary	121
PART THREE Imagination Made Real	**123**
6 Entrepreneur	**125**
Value pricing	126
Partnerships	128
Opportunities	132
Trust	134
Toolkit to success	138
Summary	141
7 Dream	**143**
Financial freedom	144
Goals	147
Vision	151
Repeat	152
Summary	156
Conclusion	**157**
Acknowledgements	**161**
The Author	**163**

Foreword

With access to social media and *Dragon's Den*, many people think the life of an entrepreneur is only for a niche group of people – the Bill Gateses and Richard Bransons of this world. That can be an intimidating thought, but as Melanie rightly points out, an entrepreneur is actually 'a person who makes money by starting or running businesses, especially when this involves financial risk'. Therefore, many of us either are or aspire to be entrepreneurs.

In this book, Melanie lays bare the journey that we embark upon to become entrepreneurs and helps us find the quickest way to success. Making that journey as direct as possible means we achieve success sooner, profit earlier and experience less pain along the way than those who meander.

I met Melanie a few years ago when she demystified my tax returns and, by doing so, removed a significant level of stress from my life. Melanie's passion for what she does drives her to empower people to follow their dreams of self-employment. When I discussed with her the possibility of me becoming self-employed, she explained the constituent parts, offering suggestions and solutions. Working with so many people who have embarked on this somewhat intimidating journey, she has developed an extensive understanding of the issues and, equally importantly, the people themselves: what drives them, their fears and their ambitions.

In *Unlock the Entrepreneur Within*, her belief and personal drive are palpable, and yet she has a true humility. She knows the power of hard work and that a mentor can bring a strong sense of accountability to enterprises, reducing the likelihood of procrastination. Her open mindset looks at the potential for something positive in every situation, yet she has balance. Refreshingly, she understands and addresses fear of failure and being overwhelmed, and acknowledges the reality that not everyone will be supportive. Those people closest to us may not see our vision, perhaps because they do not have our courage. Some may even sabotage our efforts – this is an uncomfortable fact that all of us may have to confront.

I love the way Melanie describes the goalsetting process. We all need to set big goals. Often, when we get

FOREWORD

there, we can reflect that it was not such a big deal after all. Working towards a goal takes hard work, granted, but as Melanie explains, when we approach this journey with an open mindset and the willingness to do what it takes, we put ourselves into extreme learning. With every goal we achieve, which will mean confronting the inevitable 'bumps' along the way, we move to a higher plane, forever building our knowledge pool to take on the next challenge.

While profit is great, Melanie emphasises the freedom that starting our own successful business will bring. There can be no monetary value placed on doing a job we love and finding time to do things we value. For Melanie, reward is about life satisfaction as much as profit. Inspiring others, making a difference to the next generation, to her children, is essential to her, and she has learned to do that on her own bumpy journey through the fear, hard work and exhaustion of running a business. Having learned from that journey, she is excited to share her tips and lessons with others.

I love that Melanie measures success and profit in terms of personal growth, which will not be achieved while we are in our comfort zone. Indeed, she frequently urges us to push ourselves out of the comfort zone and into the fear zone, so that we can learn and grow. Through all this, she also stresses the importance of work-life balance. Life is about more than just work, so we all need to network and develop our 'tribe', taking time to think and step back from the day-to-day running of our business. In this book, Melanie shows us how.

Karen Baxter
Director and shareholder, KPH Consultancy Ltd, and retired commander, City of London Police

Introduction

As director of M Squared Accountancy Ltd, a successful cloud-based practice, I work with both male and female entrepreneurs, most of whom are aged between thirty and sixty-five. They all have a brilliant product or service they know will significantly help others and a burning desire to take this to market. What they don't necessarily have is the knowledge or skills to turn their ideas into reality – or, more importantly, how to make money from those ideas.

Does this sound familiar? If so, this book is for you.

Whether you have a start-up or an established business that you want to take to the next level, the first thing you will need is a growth mindset. My experience of working with entrepreneurs over the past seven years has shown me that the most successful are those who are open minded. With the right mindset and the willingness to follow a plan – a roadmap to success that sets out the action you need to take at each step of the way – you will be able to achieve your goals.

Even better, once you have learned the steps to success, you can simply repeat the process to run multiple businesses simultaneously. Most people in my network have more than one business, either in a similar industry or in a completely new field. Many are making money while they sleep – an entrepreneur's dream.

I love what I do as I get to help people every day. A single mum to two amazing boys, I started my own business in my living room after being made redundant. Seven years later, I have three members of staff and over 300 clients. My gorgeous, bright, spacious office is in the heart of Lisburn city centre in Northern Ireland. In those seven years, I have experienced everything you are likely to go through and have developed a plan that will enable you to achieve what I have achieved – and more.

Many businesses fail in the first six to twelve months of their existence.[1] The reasons for this are various, from a lack of understanding of the process and the

---

1 T Carter 'The true failure rate of small businesses', *Entrepreneur* (2021), www.entrepreneur.com/article/361350, accessed 5 April 2022

steps to success to a lack of resilience and awareness of the sheer hard work involved to get a business off the ground.

Entrepreneurs on YouTube and Instagram living the 'laptop life' on the beach and saying they only work two to three hours a day paint a misleading picture. They can lull us in to believing it is going to be easy, so when we don't achieve results quickly, we tend to become overwhelmed by the feeling that we must be all things to all people at the same time. Large companies have chief executive officers, sales and marketing directors, accountants and production managers as well as employees to carry out the day-to-day tasks. As entrepreneurs founding or running a small business, usually due to lack of budget and/or resources, we need to wear all these hats ourselves.

Before long, we realise that there are not enough hours in the day to do everything we want or need to do, let alone sit on the beach or go bungee jumping or snowboarding or whatever else the laptop-life entrepreneurs get up to. We find we are not making any money as our business is in chaos, and after a few months, we hit a wall and suffer from burnout.

Some of us may get to the point where we believe that going back to full-time employment is a much safer option than running our own business. There, we can get a regular income and a specific task to complete each day and leave the stress of running the business to someone else. After all, we have the same bills to pay as we did before we started our own business and, of course, a certain lifestyle to maintain. With only 3% of the population doing what we are doing,[2] employment looks like the favourable alternative. However, those 3% earn 97% of all money earned.

The truth is, financial freedom is possible. The laptop life is possible, but only if you have an open mindset to follow the steps to success I have outlined in this book.

When I started my business, I didn't have a mentor to point me in the right direction and keep me focused. I had to learn quickly about my own strengths and weaknesses and use my qualities to my advantage. I now have many mentors who I connect with as soon as I have a query. I act on their advice, solve the problem within minutes and move another step towards achieving my goal. My mentors rescue me from weeks of dilemmas, not only saving me money, but also allowing me to get a lot more done in one day and spend more quality time with my boys to help develop their goals.

Many people believe that you need to be born an entrepreneur, but you do not. You can learn the skills you need and, with the right knowledge and understanding, build a successful business. I have a wealth

---

2   S Gallagher, '5 steps to creating multiple sources of income' (Proctor Gallagher Institute, no date), www.proctorgallagherinstitute.com/25811/5-steps-to-creating-multiple-sources-of-income, accessed 18 May 2022

INTRODUCTION

of experience to share with you as you go through each stage of your business journey. Using my step-by-step guide to entrepreneurship, you will learn and grow as you come ever closer to achieving your goals.

Many people in business spend too much time comparing themselves to others in their industry. It is good to notice what others are doing, but not to give it too much attention. Far better to be in competition with yourself, to look at your current results and see how you can improve them.

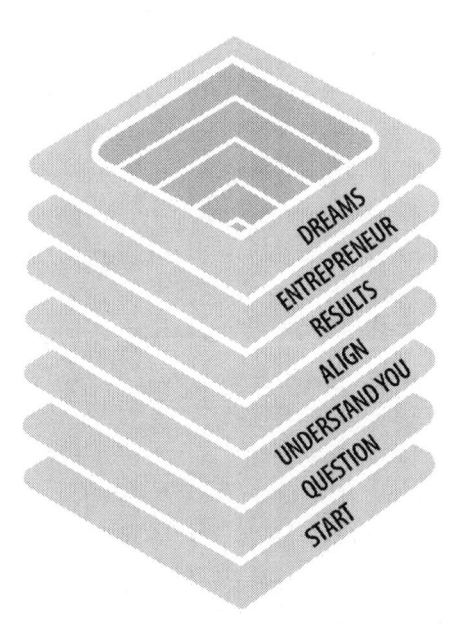

DREAMS
ENTREPRENEUR
RESULTS
ALIGN
UNDERSTAND YOU
QUESTION
START

To keep you focused and give you direction to become a successful entrepreneur, I have developed the SQUARED model, which is made up of seven steps:

1. **S**tart
2. **Q**uestion
3. **U**nderstand you
4. **A**lign
5. **R**esults
6. **E**ntrepreneur
7. **D**reams

We will cover the first two steps in Part One, 'Where To Begin'. In Part Two, 'Changing Your Mindset, we will explore steps three to five; then we will finish with steps six and seven in Part Three, 'Imagination Made Real'. The SQUARED model gives you a roadmap to follow, showing you why you may struggle at some stages more than at others. I have gone through this process many times myself over the past seven years and will continue to do so as I break through each level of growth.

An entrepreneur's journey can be an emotional one that takes many twists and turns before you reach your final destination. With a detailed plan, combined with hard work and support, you are on the verge of arguably the most exciting time of your life.

Let's start this journey together.

PART ONE
WHERE TO BEGIN

1
Start

In this chapter, we will look at where you currently are in your life and business, and where you want to get to. We will discover the reasons why we as entrepreneurs sometimes stay still and don't move forward with something, even though we have the burning desire to do so. We will learn why we can become overwhelmed and what we can do to prevent this from happening.

It can be scary to make yourself vulnerable and open to scrutiny. This first step of the SQUARED model will teach you that while other people may want to give you their opinion, you are the one who decides whether to accept or reject it.

Feeling stuck and overwhelmed

The word 'entrepreneur' comes from the French word *entreprendre* meaning 'take on'. As business owners, we are met with challenges to take on at every turn. We have two choices: we can either run away or face each challenge head on. Sometimes, we may perceive an obstacle as too big to overcome, but when we decide to face it, the stretch in our growth is huge.

Facing up to obstacles in our way can feel painful, both emotionally and physically. We may feel overwhelmed, wanting to go back to our comfort zone where everything is familiar, but to break through the terror barrier and reap the rewards on the other side, we have to experience these growing pains.

The first thing we're all likely to do is look at those closest to us for support, asking them for their opinion. Entrepreneur, motivational speaker and author Jim Rohn famously suggested that we are an average of the five people we spend most of our time with. This is significant at this point in your journey.[3]

As those closest to us care for us deeply, they do not want to see us in pain. They may be fearful that entrepreneurship will change us so much that they will be left behind, so they advise us to stop what we are

---

[3] A Groth, 'You're the average of the five people you spend the most time with', *Insider* (2012), www.businessinsider.com/jim-rohn-youre-the-average-of-the-five-people-you-spend-the-most-time-with-2012-7, accessed 18 May 2022

doing. They tell us not to take out that loan or invest in that business. We know they care and we're likely to believe that they are being supportive, so we take their advice.

What we really tend to be seeking at this start point in the journey is the approval of those around us. We want them to take away from us the decision to move forward with the venture. This way if it fails, it is on them and not on us. We can then make excuses that ours was not the right product or service, or it was not the right time to start a business.

Beware of this mindset; there is *no wrong time to start a business*. For proof, we just need to look at the array of creative businesses that popped up during the Covid-19 pandemic and remain successful to this day.

When we desperately want the approval of a loved one, it is our head fighting with our heart. Take an example of going to view a dream house. Our heart tells us this is the perfect home for us, but our head immediately looks at the monthly mortgage repayments and our logical side kicks in. Before we know it, we're bombarding ourselves with all the reasons why we should not buy it.

Despite the relentless flow of logical arguments against buying that house, something keeps drawing us back to it. Somehow, we find the money for the deposit and, further down the line, the monthly repayments.

It's the same with starting our own business. The business owner that we admire probably spends a lot of quality time with their loved ones. They have more than one holiday a year, live in a lovely mortgage-free house and drive a beautiful car. Perhaps they are not a millionaire, but they seem genuinely happy.

We then reflect on our own lives: how busy we are; how we have no free time; how we are always tired. We may experience broken sleep as we worry about everything we need to do the next day, so we have no energy during the day. Too tired to cook in the evenings, we end up having too many takeaways. We may often be in a bad mood, impatient with our loved ones and unable to see a way off the hamster wheel.

Most entrepreneurs who have not been born into a family of business owners feel like this, but there *is* a way off that wheel. You just need to think like an entrepreneur and ask yourself some hard-hitting questions:

- Are you willing and able to make the necessary changes to enable your goal to happen?
- Are you willing to let your heart lead you?
- Do you trust your own judgement?

- Are you willing to lose some friends along the way if they are no longer aligned with your goals?
- Do you need a mentor to guide and support you?

If the answer is *yes* to all of these questions, then you have already started your journey.

When you're faced with each challenge along the way, you are likely to ask yourself these questions many times over. You may wonder how much you really want financial freedom, to be happy and spend quality time with your family. The answer is simple. *If* you have made the decision to grow – if you continue to answer yes to the questions – then you are prepared to do the hard work necessary to make the changes.

I have been through this journey myself and I can say hand on heart it has been in equal measure the best and most difficult journey I have ever undertaken. I can also say it has been the most exciting and scariest one, and it has allowed me the most growth. I have met interesting, supportive, likeminded people along the way and made friends for life.

I have travelled to different countries on business retreats and training courses: countries that I would never have experienced if I were still working in my nine-to-five job. I have completed many creative projects and I manage my activities rather than my time. Best of all, I have repeated the process, setting up new business ventures to maximise my growth.

CASE STUDY: HARRY HOXSEY

The story of Harry Hoxsey is a great example of true entrepreneurship, illustrating how going against the grain and following your heart against all odds is the key to success.

From 1921, Hoxsey opened clinics throughout the USA so he could reach as many people as possible with his cure for all forms of cancer.[4] He came up against a lot of scrutiny and people calling him a quack, and he was arrested many times, but the police had to release him as they had no grounds to charge him. On one occasion when he was due to be arrested, his patients circled his building to stop the authorities from entering.

Based on his extensive research, Hoxsey knew in his heart that his tonic was curing people and he had to get the word out across the world so that no one would have to suffer again. He met with government officials and agreed to sell his patent so that they could spread the word, but just prior to signing, they told him they would bury his patent and no one would know about his treatment. At the eleventh hour, Hoxsey refused to sign his patent over to the US government, instead ordering his head nurse to take the tonic and open a clinic in Tijuana, just across the Mexican border where the US restrictions would not apply.

Hope on the Hill, as the clinic is known today by the locals, is still operating and has become popular not

---

[4] Hoxsey Biomedical Center, 'Clinic history' (Hoxsey, no date), www.hoxseybiomedical.com/clinic-history, accessed 3 May 2022; H Hoxsey, *Hoxsey Therapy: When natural cures for cancer became illegal. The historical autobiography of Harry Hoxsey* (Transpersonal Publishing, 2010)

only with Americans who hop across the border, but with cancer sufferers right across the world. Due to its overwhelming success rate, the clinic operates on word of mouth. Harry Hoxsey's tonic is now bringing hope to people around the world, just as he dreamed it would.[5]

How to avoid the business plateau

What stage of the entrepreneurial journey are you at? Do you look at your business and see that it has grown and been successful for many years, but it has flattened out and plateaued? When you look back over the past twelve months, do you realise you have been working *in* rather than *on* your business? Do you feel like an employee of your own company? Does everyone seem to want a piece of you, so you have no time to think creatively?

Quite frankly, are you bored? Is every day the same? Was this not one of the reasons you left employment? Your business is not growing when you work in it. You want your juices to be flowing because you are thinking creatively about how to work on it.

If you look at your business from the perspective of a potential client, would you like to work with your company? Is your company forward thinking? Does it

---

5   K Asubel, 'Tempest in a tonic bottle: A bunch of weeds?', *HerbalGram*, 49 (2000), pp32–43, www.herbalgram.org/resources/herbalgram/issues/49/table-of-contents/article2270, accessed 17 May 2022

have the latest software? Does it move with the times? Do you hire the best staff? If the answer is no to any of these questions, then you need to step up your game and put the right measures in place.

Any business owner who wants to take their business to the next level needs to make a giant leap, which can often be scary. It may involve acquiring a new company, moving into a different type of business altogether, hiring a mentor or employing a marketing company or a sales director. These experts work alongside you as the owner to assess the internal controls as they stand and make the relevant changes to reduce inefficiencies.

This can cause friction if you're a business owner set in your ways and not willing to listen to advice and make the necessary changes. On the other hand, if you're a business owner who is open minded, you realise your company has flatlined and want to take the relevant action, you are far more likely to be receptive to change and growth.

If you are an open-minded individual who is willing to grow and take your company to the next level, you may need to change how you have previously run it by introducing a venture capitalist or an investor, or borrowing large sums of money for an acquisition. You may need to learn a new skill to start a business in a completely different field. Whatever approach you take, a mentor can guide you at every step of the journey.

Mentors keep you accountable through the times when you want to give up. If you do not have someone to keep you accountable when you face difficult challenges or have to make crucial decisions, you may well want to backtrack into your comfort zone. It can easily seem too hard to move forward alone.

Many entrepreneurs have experienced this temptation to backtrack – I certainly have. We start to listen to the voices in our heads and ask those closest to us for their opinion. Often, because they care about us and don't want to see us struggling, they tell us to stay where we are, that this new venture is too hard and not the right thing for us to do.

When we work with a mentor, we can direct all our questions to them as they have already experienced everything we are going through. They are the perfect person to use as a sounding board for all our fears and worries as they have felt every negative emotion and pushed through, so they can prevent us from becoming overwhelmed.

A mentor will remind us of all the reasons to move forward with our project, to follow our heart's desire rather than listen to our head and retreat into doing nothing. Doing nothing may seem to be the easier and safer option, but it's where there is no growth. If we as business owners don't move forward, we are likely to regret it for the rest of our lives, especially when we see other businesspeople succeeding with an idea that is almost identical to the one we abandoned.

It may be that you do not feel ready to work with a mentor yet, especially if their fee is outside of your current budget, but a mentor's advice is so valuable to your growth experience, it is likely to pay for itself many times over. You will save months, maybe years of trying to find a solution by yourself. The time that you save, you can spend with the ones you love or on finding creative new directions for yourself and your business.

Life can seem long, but actually, it's not. Sometimes a difficult or sad event, such as an illness or the death of a close family member, can remind us to reflect and make plans for major changes in our lives. None of us can ever know when it'll be too late, so we need to take the positive from the negative and use the painful reminders of how short life really is as a foothold on to the next step to our goals. We need to lift ourselves up and move forward rather than back to the life we had previously.

We can do this with professional and personal goals. Our results in life show where we are emotionally; there is a direct link between achieving our goals and how we feel about ourselves, and the most successful business owners in the world have made that connection. Our self-image shows up in every aspect of our lives and shines a light on the areas we need to focus on.

The most successful entrepreneurs allocate time to thinking. In other words, they spend time working *on* their business rather than *in* it. As a business owner, you constantly need to be coming up with fresh ideas to grow your business, so to get the best results, allocate a few hours each week, maybe on the same day each week if you're a creature of habit, to do a 'mind dump'.

A mind dump is where you write down all your ideas to grow your business on a sheet of paper, freeing up space in your brain to carry out the day-to-day tasks. When you work on *and* in your business at the same time, you can often end up feeling overwhelmed and doing nothing at all. After a few days have passed, come back to your mind dump list, strike off the ideas you feel are no longer viable and take action on the others. Some ideas can be implemented immediately while others take several months or even years.

Break the ones that will take a while to achieve down into small chunks that you can realistically manage each day. This way, you mitigate the risk of becoming overwhelmed. Write a list of five goal-achieving activities that you can complete in a day, for example researching a course, finding a mentor or simply setting up a meeting with someone you believe can help you move forward. These small steps may seem effortless when you're doing them, but they add up over the months. When you look back in three months' time and review what you have achieved, you are likely to be amazed and immensely proud of yourself.

What others think of you is not important, even if they are people who care about you. It's healthy to observe what other people in the same industry as you are doing, but if you give too much attention to your competitors, you take the focus off yourself and what you want to achieve. Do not get distracted by other people; if you hit a wall, go to your mentor and find the answer. Be in competition only with yourself and focus on up-levelling every single day.

Believe in yourself

You may have heard of the movie *The Greatest Showman*. It is one of the best movies to watch through the eyes of an entrepreneur, not just because of its uplifting mood, memorable music and tale of hardship to success, but because it epitomises the journey that every entrepreneur has gone through. It has been referenced at entrepreneurial events all over the world to create a feeling of excitement, motivation and empowerment.

CASE STUDY: PT BARNUM

Step into the shoes of the protagonist of *The Greatest Showman*, PT Barnum. The ultimate dreamer, he believed that someday he would be successful. Those closest to him thought he was rash, but every decision he made worked towards his end goal: to be as successful as possible and get himself out of poverty. He wanted to provide for his wife and children and give them everything he did not have as a child.

This is exactly what he did, but somewhere along the way, it all went to his head, and he became complacent, even arrogant. He stopped being grateful for what he had until he finally learned a harsh lesson: he could lose it all far more easily than he had gained it.

In a heartbeat, everything he had worked for was gone. The difference this time, though, was that he was surrounded by likeminded people who believed in him. They'd seen him do it once before and knew he could do it again, and so he did. With his family by his side, he rebuilt his empire, this time not forgetting the people he'd done it for in the first place.

Every entrepreneur has walked in similar shoes. We often have big dreams, but do not always have the confidence or support to take action towards them. PT Barnum had droves of confidence, but not necessarily the knowledge or expertise he needed. That did not stop him; he decided his dreams would become a reality. Some would call him pig-headed or stubborn, his determination that his dream would be realised seeming mad to those who did not see his vision. Others would see him as brave, leading with his heart rather than his head.

Most of us had dreams when we were children. Free from the trappings of adult reservations, we knew what felt right for us, but we didn't know how to achieve it. When we continue to follow our hearts and believe in our dreams into adulthood, somehow, we find a way to make them happen. We maybe think of others living our dream instead of us and realise just how much we want it. Once we are within reach of our goal, we feel excited, but when it happens, there are no fireworks or wild celebrations. Instead, there's just a deep feeling of satisfaction; we're impressed with ourselves. We may wonder what we made all the fuss about in the first place as we reflect on our journey, realising it wasn't that scary after all.

Within weeks of achieving one goal, we need to dream up an even bigger one. We now have the knowledge, confidence and network around us to help us on our quest, so we repeat the process while delving into a new area of growth.

You do the same with your business. Once you are on a higher vibration, you do not want to stay at that level. Instead, use that as your starting point for growth. You may speak to angel investors, capital investors or property developers, take training on the stock markets or investigate franchising your business. You may trademark your name or product to avoid others copying and replicating your idea. You may form a limited company to protect your assets. You may invest in more mentors to help you decide what you want to achieve next. People buy from people, so once you start networking with the right people, you will naturally be drawn to the experts in your field who have your best interests at heart. You may investigate multiple sources of income or letting out a property to obtain passive income.

The list is endless once you open your mind. Money is not to be feared, but revered. In many countries, it is classed as rude to talk about money in public, but the reality is, money makes the world go round and tends to be an entrepreneur's favourite topic. When you scrutinise numbers on your balance sheet, you can improve on your own targets. You are in competition with yourself and can only improve if you have your own comparative figures as your starting block. There are enough clients for every business, so don't concern yourself with how your competitors are doing. Once you accept this to be true, you are likely to be at peace with yourself. All the abilities and competitiveness you need are within you already.

CASE STUDY: HELPING A BUSINESS GROW EXPONENTIALLY

A client approached me last year with a problem she was having within her business, which had been growing successfully over the past five years. She wanted to achieve exponential growth by purchasing another business in the same field as hers but didn't know where to start or how to go about the process, so she came to me for advice.

She signed up to my twelve-week mentoring programme that would take her through the process from start to finish. It would show her methodically what to do and how to do it so things didn't become overwhelming for her, and she could streamline the process quickly to achieve her end goal. We looked at the legal matters, physical location, staff, costs and internal mechanism to ensure that as we hit every milestone, she would grow within herself as well as being able to deal with the exponential business growth.

After twelve weeks, when she had completed the programme, she realised just how far she had come in such a short space of time. She had found larger premises and hired staff to service the hundreds of new clients, and the people around her were taking notice of the changes in not only her business life, but her personal life too. People in the same business as her started to come to her for advice, something she had never believed would happen.

Fear of growth

Some entrepreneurs have as much fear of growth as they do of failure. Their business has got off the ground and become relatively successful. They pay their taxes but are happy to stay under the higher tax threshold and keep their business small. The business is well known in the local area; it has regular clients who give it repeat custom, good feedback and recommendations.

This business is doing OK, but it could be amazing. It could be selling goods all around the world on Amazon or eBay, making the owner money while they sleep; it could be a household name.

Ask yourself this question: are you afraid to grow? You may feel that your product or service is not good enough to have worldwide appeal. You may believe *you* are not good enough as you do not have the knowledge or skills to mass produce your product. If you look at the people around you, you may worry that business growth will change you. Will your friends and family look at you differently? Will they believe that you think you are better than them? Do you feel you don't deserve a nice car or large home?

One thing is true: the more you grow as a businessperson, the more you will become exposed. If this makes you feel vulnerable, that's only natural, but exposure is part of growth, so think of it as a good thing. It's better to accept it rather than ignore it or fight it.

Once you work out why you feel a certain way, this disarms the feeling almost immediately, so look inwards and find the reasons behind your insecurities. You can do this by using a healing modality such as the Energy Alignment Method (EAM) or Energy Freedom Therapy (EFT), otherwise known as tapping.[6] Talking it through with a mentor or journaling your fears and insecurities and the reasons for them are other ways to release the stuck emotions held deep within your body.

The main thing to keep in mind is that all behaviours are learned. This means they can also be unlearned, which is where the magic happens. When you have some 'Aha!' moments, you are likely to feel the shift in your mindset, releasing a bit of energy that was stuck and immediately feeling lighter, happier and more confident. You can now move your focus from the problem to the solution, allowing you to move to the next level of growth. As you hit each milestone, you become aware of your emotions, and you continue to release and grow at each stage until you reach your final target. You then create a new goal and repeat the process.

After a few months, the negative chatter in your head will be dulled. It is at this point that most people stop caring what others think of them. When you get to this point, you're free to try new things, experience new adventures and attract a higher level of client. Once those clients are delighted by your product or service, they will refer you to their friends, family and

---

6   See www.energyalignmentmethod.com and www.eftdownunder.com/energy-techniques/what-is-emotional-freedom-techniques-eft

business associates, and before you know it, you'll be hiring more staff to meet the demand.

When you are happy in your own skin, you are likely to be healthy, sleep well, eat well and use the extra energy this creates to improve other aspects of your life. This is infectious – before long, the people around you will be making improvements in their lives. Remember, they too are the average of the people they spend most time with, and if one of those people is the new improved you, they will inevitably benefit.

When you have the time and opportunity to learn about yourself and what makes you tick, such as what you really like and your core beliefs and boundaries, you are better equipped to decide what you will put up with and what you won't. You can strive to be a better version of yourself and respect yourself more, and those around you will treat you accordingly.

Once you are in this place of confidence and clarity, you're in a position to grow your business organically. Before long, you'll not only be in the higher tax bracket, you'll be registering your business for VAT – and, believe it or not, probably embracing it because you'll no longer feel scared or vulnerable. If you do not know how to do something, you can employ more mentors to help you. Then you can pay it forward and tell everyone about your own experience to save them years of hard work, money and time.

CASE STUDY: JOY MANGANO

Joy Mangano is an American entrepreneur who, in 1990, developed a self-wringing mop after becoming frustrated with ordinary mops. She invested her savings and borrowed money from family and friends, desperate to get her mop out to the masses. Following her heart, she believed that her product would be a success.

She eventually got enough money to make a prototype and sold 1,000 mops. She went to trade shows, where the mop was picked up by the shopping channel QVC. It sold modestly until Joy went on the shopping channel herself. Having freed herself from her doubts and insecurities, she was able to let her confidence in her product and herself shine through, and in the first hour, she had sold a whopping 18,000 mops, more than she could ever have imagined.

Within twelve months, Joy had incorporated her business as Arma Products. By the year 2000, the company was selling $10m worth of Miracle Mops per year.

Fear of failure

As much as we may fear succeeding, many of us have an equal fear of failing. Some of us may leave a job, telling all our friends and family what our new business venture is going to be and how we are going to make lots of money and take over the world. When things don't take off or they go wrong, we feel embarrassed that we talked so openly about succeeding and want to hide from everyone who put their trust in us.

Some of us may put all our eggs into one basket and partner with a company promising us high investment terms that do not materialise. If we don't do all the research we should about a company before partnering with it, it may fail within a few months, leaving us high and dry.

Some of us may start our own business without having any previous entrepreneurial experience, thinking it will be good fun, but we soon find out the hard way where our shortfalls are. If we don't review the market, reconcile our figures and keep a close eye on our targets, we may well introduce a poor product to a nonexistent customer base. Maybe we make some money, but being inexperienced, we draw it out of the company and spend it on having fun rather than reinvesting it in the form of staff, software or training. With dwindling resilience, confidence and funds, we are likely to be dissolving our business sooner rather than later.

A company formed on poor foundations with poor internal controls will ultimately fail. It can only survive if growth happens slowly and we as the founder make changes to products, processes and systems along the way whenever problems arise. Sometimes a business becomes an overnight success, and this can bring its own problems if the company overtrades and cannot meet the demand of its consumers. Maybe it doesn't have the correct ordering system to receive the high level of bookings or enough trained operatives to resolve customer-service issues or make its product. Unsatisfied clients soon move to a different supplier.

To avoid your company being among the many that fail, make consistency an important factor throughout its life. As a business owner, you must lead your team with clear and concise directions. Remember, your vision is only in your mind's eye until you have made your team aware of it so they can work in line with your core values. A company mission and vision statement that everyone adheres to is essential. Give your team clarity on what you want to achieve at all times.

If you work in opposition to your inner values, you instil confusion within your company. Your staff and clients alike will feel your confusion, which causes a lack of trust. Clients disengage, investors withdraw funds, staff move to a different company and your business goes into decline. If you do not rectify this with all haste, your business will fold.

Branding is as essential to you personally as it is to your company. People buy from people, so if there is an imbalance between your personal and business branding, this causes confusion and mistrust. Personal branding is about more than your letterheads matching your business cards and website. It is when your morals and core values are rolled out into your business ethos. Your thoughts and beliefs are displayed in everything you and your company do, your actions match your words, and your staff are in line with your vision. If it were possible, you would feel, talk and even dress like your business. Your energy is aligned with its energy, and this carries through into your results.

When you work with people or companies that don't align with your values, you are setting yourself up for failure. In the confusion created by the misalignment, the people you deal with won't be interested in helping you.

Without any direction, you will drift through life. This applies to your business as much as it does to your personal life. If you do not have an exact plan of where you are heading, you are likely to fail or give up when the times get tough; and you can be sure that you will face difficult times. Anything worth having requires hard work, stepping out of your comfort zone and growth.

Roadmap to success

You can make your growth as easy or as hard as you want. If you decide to go through it alone, with the right mindset, you will succeed, but you will be making it harder for yourself than it needs to be. If you have support, usually in the form of a mentor, you make the process much easier. When you work with a mentor, you will move in leaps and bounds towards your chosen goal. This may shave months, if not years, off the time it takes to achieve your goal.

The first thing I advise my clients to do when I'm mentoring them is to choose their goals, one for their personal life and one for their professional life. Write down your purpose for achieving your goals so you can make an emotional connection with them. Maybe you want to spend more time with your family, travel or enjoy the finer things in life. Whatever the purpose is for you, connect each goal to the emotion it evokes. This is your *why*, your reason for choosing this goal over others.

You then reverse engineer your goal back to the present day to give yourself a starting point. From this starting point, before you go to bed, write a list of activities to carry out the next day. A plan of action is then likely to manifest in your subconscious mind throughout the night and all the hard work will be done by the time you wake in the morning. The next day, you can set to work on your goal-achieving activities. That evening, you repeat the process and sleep on a plan for the following day, and so on.

As repetition is key to forming a new habit, you may want to give up many times; it can become boring doing the same thing every day. Bear in mind that any pain you are feeling now will be worth it in the end. You will learn how to be resilient and patient, qualities that will be essential as you experience each level of growth.

You will also need to reverse engineer the amount of money you wish to earn annually. Once you decide what your new annual income will be, bring this back to what you need to earn in a month, a week and each day. This detail is extremely important to keep you on track with your goal.

Choosing a date to achieve a goal by is essential to lock in the fact that you are taking the goal seriously, you mean business and have no intentions of wavering off your path. Make the date you choose realistic. If you choose a big goal that needs a year, but only give yourself a month to get it done, you'll almost certainly conclude that your goal is not achievable and give up. At the other end of the scale, if you choose a date that is too far in the future, you may lose interest. The date you choose must be relative to the size of your goal, but don't worry too much if you don't meet the deadline. Don't give up – keep going until you complete the goal.

EXERCISE: THE WHEEL OF LIFE

A part of my business that I enjoy the most is mentoring my clients. When I see the difference in people at the end compared to where they started, it makes me proud. I have been able to give them the tools to change, but they have done the hard work because they made the decision to do so.

As I do with my clients when they are at the start of their journey, I advise you to complete the Wheel of Life model to assess your current position in each area of your life.[7] Invented in the 1960s by Paul J Meyer, the wheel covers many areas of life – for example, health, money, relationships, spiritual, contribution, personal development, surroundings and fun – and gives you a real indication of how you see yourself. This, in turn, provides a good overview of which areas of your life you are happy with and which areas you need to improve.

To complete your own Wheel of Life, draw out the wheel below – you could draw around a circular object or trace this version.

Starting with the area where you feel you want to make the biggest change, work through each section, scoring your level of satisfaction with that area of your life, with 10 being completely fulfilled and 1 being totally discontented. Circle the number in each section of the wheel that represents your satisfaction level, with ten, at the border of the wheel, being the most satisfied you can be:

---

[7] M Schrager 'Parallels – Life wheel for you and your organization' (Systems of Change, 2016), https://systemsofchange.com/parallels-life-wheel-organization, accessed 5 April 2022

START

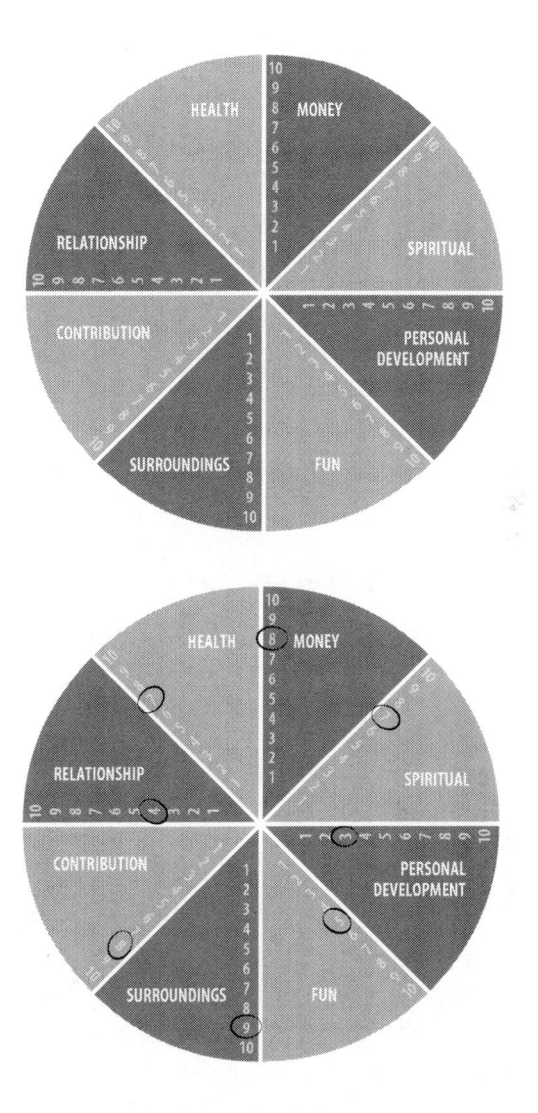

Once you can see the different levels, choose one section in which you'd like to be more fulfilled. Set yourself a goal that when achieved will improve your score for this area of your life.

Summary

In this chapter, we looked at where you are today and where you plan to be in the future. We examined how the people around you may be holding you back, even with the best of intentions, and how a mentor can really accelerate your growth. You now know that it's possible you're as afraid of success as you may be of failure. With a basic understanding of why you are where you are and what you need to do to make changes, you can create momentum and get ahead in your life.

You need to take full responsibility for your actions and learn from your life so far so you can recognise what is holding you back. Once you have clarity on your own vision and mission, you need to convey that clarity to those around you, so they are aligned with your values.

The start of your entrepreneurial journey is an exciting place to be. Once you make the changes necessary for growth, you will become an influencer in both your business and personal life as others see the improvements you're making and become inspired to improve themselves.

2
Question

In this chapter, we will look inwards and ask questions that you may never have thought about before. It's likely that you'll be able to answer some of these questions straight away; some may need a bit longer to figure out. Take time to work through each question and you will learn so much about yourself.

We as human beings are social creatures who thrive on the energy from others. When we know who we are, what we like and don't like, we can set our boundaries and present ourselves as confident and authentic.

What is your why?

How did you get to where you are today? Look back over your life and identify each significant step that led you to the here and now. Most people have a reason why they do what they do, but few take the time to reflect on the path that led them there.

As an entrepreneur, you have a unique story that no one can replicate. You may have been born into a family of entrepreneurs, but most people do not have this luxury. Many start a business when they are made redundant or on maternity leave and can't see a way of raising a family within the strict boundaries of employment.

When you have a product or service that you truly believe will sell and you follow your heart to bring it to the marketplace, this gives you a growth mindset right from the start. Coupling this growth mindset with a strong why and your unique story, you give yourself and your business the best chance to succeed.

Be accountable to yourself and do what it takes to make success happen. Mentors are great at helping to keep you accountable. Put in the work needed. Push yourself out of your comfort zone to learn a new skill, sign up for networking events, listen to inspirational speakers and surround yourself with likeminded people, but in the end, only you can make sure your business succeeds.

You may be surprised by how creative you can be with your ideas once you have clarity on your why. There are no limits to what you can achieve when you are passionate about what you are doing. Others may tell you your ideas are crazy, but you'll know you are on the right path and they are simply too afraid to do what you are doing. When you end up making money from what feels like a hobby, from something you love, you'll never be left wondering what all your hard work in life was actually for.

Life is meant to be fun. With the right mindset that comes from having a strong why behind you, you can have anything you desire. You'll change your focus from making others happy to making yourself happy, which isn't as selfish a concept as it sounds.

When you make yourself happy by doing the things you love, you lead by example and others start to do the same. You become more independent and confident, which attracts clients to you, so you stop needing people in your life and instead work with the ones who are truly aligned with your values. All this is achievable by doing something you are passionate about.

When you love what you do, your positivity radiates to those closest to you. You're likely to jump out of bed every morning, keen to start your day. The reason to follow your heart and your why and work at doing something you love may not be to get material items, but they do tend to be a nice bonus. Life simply becomes more enjoyable. You have less stress and worry and can focus on what really matters, such as the people you love.

Many entrepreneurs talk about money and make money, but is money the reason they do what they do? From my experience, money is usually a by-product of success. If you are happy in your work, you can have many projects on the go at the same time, some of them making money for you while you sleep. With an abundance of energy and passion, you will be able to give as much to multiple projects as you can to one.

If you have never had a mentor or been in the vicinity of a self-made millionaire, you may wonder if this is really possible. Do you believe only people born into riches and fame can do things like this? Is this lifestyle for everyone else, but not for you? Do you believe rich people are different to you? That they are better than you? That they are just lucky?

This is not the case. When you study people like Richard Branson, Grant Cardone and Gary Vaynerchuk, you'll see what they all tend to have in common: they have learned about themselves; they love themselves; they know what makes them tick. They have strict boundaries and a healthy relationship with money, but more significantly than anything else, they do not believe they are better than you or me.

CASE STUDY: WE ALL NEED A REASON TO GET OUT OF BED IN THE MORNING

A client approached me for support several years ago. She wanted to change for the better but couldn't pinpoint why she'd felt low for most of her adult life.

She worked in full-time employment, which she no longer enjoyed or felt passionate about. Undervalued or ignored by her work colleagues, she felt invisible in most areas of her life. She was truly miserable and dreaded the alarm going off each morning as she struggled to face the day; she knew she could not continue in this way and needed to make major changes.

When we had our first conversation, I listened intently to what she was saying about the people in her life, but to get to the root of the problem, I needed to bypass the surface-level issues. After a while, she admitted that she had always wanted to work for herself but didn't feel it was the right time in her life. Her children were young, and she felt she would be selfish to risk her financial stability and their security.

We talked through many scenarios and came up with a solution that I knew would work for her. Then we put an action plan in place. I helped her to stay accountable every step of the way.

After a year, she achieved her goal of leaving her full-time employment to become a sole trader business owner in a field she is passionate about. She is now so much happier in her own skin and can collect her children from school every day – something she had always wanted but couldn't do beforehand. She takes her family on holiday every year, something that she couldn't afford to do in the past due to her low income and high childcare costs.

Today, she is a different woman. She practises self-care, which is so important for her wellbeing. She is making money doing something she loves and is clear on her why. Best of all, her relationship with her children is better than it has ever been as they now spend so much quality time together.

How do you grow?

Do you have the desire to be successful, but have no idea where to begin? Are you new to starting a business? Do you not have anyone to call on for advice or support? Do you feel alone?

If you look online for support, you are likely to see the word 'mentor' come up time and time again. You'll have seen it a few times already in this book, but what exactly is a mentor and how can they help?

A good mentor will get you to your goal as quickly as is viably possible. They will hold you accountable at each step of your journey and will help you when you feel stuck, scared to move forward or overwhelmed. Your mentor will draw up your roadmap to success and support you on that journey. When necessary, if they can't help you solve your problem themselves, they will introduce you to people in their network who can.

You may have seen people starting the journey towards their goals, but then they lose momentum partway through. Why does that happen? Do you assume that if failure happened to them, it can happen to you?

The truth is, we all have the tools within ourselves to go all the way on our journey to success. These tools allow us to get to know ourselves at a deep level, which is essential as we navigate each dilemma we face, but without the support of a mentor to guide us through the rocky road, we can become derailed. The issues that arise may then seem so overwhelming and big that we retreat into the safety of our comfort zone.

Moving towards a goal may feel like the scariest thing you have ever done. You may even feel physically sick the first time you do it because you have never experienced such fear before. Don't worry; that's normal and the process will be much less daunting thereafter. When you repeat it several times, you'll come to understand your emotions better and better.

Once you have achieved your goal, you can analyse the process. This is where you'll understand that the growth within yourself came not in achieving the goal, but in working towards it. The steps you took along the way introduced you to experiences you would never otherwise have had. You're likely to feel differently within and about yourself, proud of yourself, maybe realising you are a stronger person than you gave yourself credit for. Once you know what you are capable of, you can do anything you put your mind to. With the right support, there are no bounds to what you can achieve.

Within a short space of time, while in this positive and confident mindset, set yourself another bigger goal. You want to achieve even more growth than the previous time, so make sure your next goal scares you more than the last. Repeat the creative process we discussed in the previous chapter of coming up with your desired goal and believing that it is truly possible, relating it to your why to ensure you're emotionally attached to it, then taking action in the form of baby steps. Before you know it, you'll be halfway along the process for a second time.

There will always be bumps in the road in all aspects of life, personal or business. Having a goal to work towards can take your mind off times that may seem difficult or challenging and drain your energy. When you redirect your focus towards your goal, you can turn a situation that could otherwise cause you anxiety and stress into a positive one. Where the focus goes, your energy goes, so when you're working towards a goal, you feel the shift within yourself and turn negative energy into positive.

QUESTION

Are you confident at making decisions?

As an entrepreneur, are you confident in the decisions you make? Once you have decided to move forward with an idea, do you rarely or never change direction?

If you find the decision-making process difficult at first, you're not alone, but all you need to do is follow your heart. You instinctively know what is right; you just have to trust that you do. Rest assured, once you have done it several times, you'll see results happen before your eyes. Then your confidence will build as you realise you *can* make good decisions without needing to get the approval of others around you and you will enjoy the results more quickly than before. Your sales and bank balance are likely to increase. Friends and family may see a positive change in you and ask what you are doing differently, making comments on how inspirational you are and positive suggestions on how you can do more, be more and expand more. They then become your biggest supporters and spread the word about your successes and business ventures. Your confidence will grow further still when you see how proud they are of you.

When you gain more clients, you need to set yourself higher monthly and yearly targets, which will make use of your newly developed decision-making skills. You can then adapt the same principles to all parts of your life, self-analysing and challenging everything you thought you knew and believed about yourself and making the decision to change anything that no longer serves you. Before you know it, you will be succeeding in all parts of your life and perfectly happy in your own skin.

Positivity is an essential part of life. It indicates that your life has meaning and that dreams are there for the taking. When you have negative thoughts, you make negative decisions, attract negative people into your life, and drama and unhappiness will follow you around.

Making a decision, even if it's the wrong one, still moves you forward. You can course-correct at any point; the key is to decide to do it quickly without any negative self-talk. Sometimes, you may feel uncomfortable about deciding until you have more information. A little research is no bad thing at all, but it can easily lead to an information overload and leave you with too much to consider and no idea which way to turn. The likely outcome is that you will remain static, moving neither forward nor backwards. What you need now is advice from a mentor who will push you out of your comfort zone.

Always do *something* rather than nothing. Even a wrong decision is at least a decision in some shape or form, and it gets you moving. Constant movement creates energy, which is where ideas are born. Ideas fire up the excitement in your belly.

People who never make decisions procrastinate and waste time, sometimes months or even years. If you're on the wrong path or in the wrong relationship, a simple decision can course correct in seconds. With practice, you will be making decisions without seeking the approval of others, which is a great place to be. It's then you will know for sure that all the answers to your questions are already within.

Who can you ask for help?

Are you the type of person who asks for help as soon as possible to solve a problem or would you rather ponder and procrastinate for weeks or months? Do you believe that if you work through the problem yourself, you will save face? Do you fear looking stupid if you don't already know the answer?

The fact is we are all learning all the time, but our egos often get in the way of us moving forward. We hold ourselves back by not taking that course, going on that retreat to learn about ourselves or meeting new people who could teach us skills we have never experienced before. We stop ourselves from studying a new language so we can move to another country, often because we care too much about what other people think of us.

Other people's opinion of you is none of your business. Once you realise this and believe it in your heart, you will be able to live your authentic life.

To be a successful entrepreneur, you need to strive to be the best version of yourself. To do this, remove your ego from the equation and turn your attention to the success of your business. Employ staff who are smarter than you so you can create a team of innovative people you can turn to whenever you are stuck and need to ask for help. Their skills will complement yours so you can offer a wide range of products or services which appeal to a high-value client in a diverse marketplace. To keep the best people on your staff, reward them with freedom and the flexibility to learn, grow and, essentially, make mistakes. It is in failure where the most growth occurs.

If you are constantly playing it safe, you are soon likely to get bored and your clients will pick up on your negative energy. When you are growing, both personally and professionally, your energy stays high and positive, and you attract the right type of clients. You become the expert in your field, the go-to person. No one can do what you do because no one has had your life experiences, walked in your shoes or learned everything that you know.

When you first start your business, it can often seem like there are not enough hours in the day to achieve what you want to achieve. Be realistic about this and

QUESTION

work with people who are willing to roll up their sleeves and help where necessary. Children, friends and family who can see your vision as clearly as you do are the best people to help until you have the resources to build your team.

You do not need people around you who complain or are jealous of your bravery as their only intention is to hold you back. People who are really on your side will do anything you need them to do for the time it takes to get your business off the ground, so don't be afraid to ask them to make up products, carry packages to the post office or take pictures for your website. This frees up your time to get the word out to potential clients and position yourself on top of the marketplace while showing the people closest to you that you are resilient, brave and strong enough to become a success and make them proud of you. If you have children, you can use this time to teach them skills that they won't learn in school, motivating them to follow their dreams as they share in your success.

Children are the best helpers when it comes to entrepreneurship. They are like sponges, watching and learning from everything you do. They see the highs and the lows and celebrate with you as you achieve each of your goals. When they reap the rewards with you, you may hear them talking about the business they would like to open one day. You are their inspiration, just as they are the reason you work so hard.

We have already covered the importance of having the right mentors by your side. In addition to mentors, a marketing team is a smart and efficient way to grow your business at an exponential rate. Hire a team that understands your values and your ideal clients, and they'll create call-to-action activities which attract a high lead generation. When you find yourself with more clients than you thought possible, the marketing team effectively pays for itself.

Funding can be an issue when you're starting out, but there are many grants you can ask for; you just need to know where to look. The most popular places are crowdfunding platforms such as GoFundMe and your local department of finance. Councils tend to offer free programmes that will create a website for you or give you the advice you require.

If you have a business plan, you can take it to the bank to request funding for growth. There are free programmes that will write your business plan for you, such as Go For It in Northern Ireland.[8] Many local councils also offer support with business plans as part of business mentoring programmes. Venture capitalists and angel investors can help to generate money quickly, but they will require a percentage of your business in return or set a high return-on-investment rate to lend you money while covering their level of risk. Ask your mentor or network about this type of funding as the route to entry can be quite involved.

---

8   www.goforitni.com

Outsourcing is another way to get help with your business. Many business owners use virtual assistants to carry out tasks that they no longer want to do themselves, giving them more time to focus on the essentials such as getting more sales and growing the business. Virtual assistants can carry out administration and bookkeeping tasks, arrange meetings and set up systems, generally taking the small tasks that are part of the day-to-day running of the business away from you. This allows you to shift your focus from working *in* the business to working *on* the business. The resultant creativity and growth make for an exciting environment to work in.

CASE STUDY: ASKING FOR SUPPORT

Three years ago, I decided to invest in a mentor for my accountancy business. I examined what I wanted to achieve and questioned why I needed one, realising I could cut out a year of small growth and fast-track myself to the next level in a short space of time with the help of a mentor.

I spent some time looking for the right fit for me: someone who understood my needs and was going to hold me accountable. They had to have walked in my shoes and be creative and logical at the same time, ie both left and right brained.

When I made my choice, I knew from that day forward my life was going to change for the better. It was exciting and scary at the same time, but it wasn't long before I was shocked when I looked back on my progress to see how far I had come. If I can do this, you can too.

How big are your goals?

What exactly does it mean for you to set a goal? For an entrepreneur, a goal is a future marker for you to strive towards. It gives you a purpose and adds meaning and direction to your life. Instead of drifting from one dream to the next and not achieving even the smallest of things, you will be on the path to success. Each small goal-achieving action you complete takes you a step closer to the end.

Goals can take weeks, months or even years to complete. If you engage a mentor, though, you will achieve your goals faster than those who do not. An accountability partner checks in on your progress; if you do not meet a deadline or milestone, they will encourage you to keep going. They keep you on track and digging deep, even when you feel that everything is against you. When you do get stuck, they will help you break down the obstacle until you can move through to the next stage.

A good mentor will ask you to select a goal that you are passionate about and follow your heart to decide on it. You use your head to set and take action steps towards your goal, but always allow your heart to choose the goal. Ideally, your mentor will help you to put an approximate timeframe on achieving your goal. If you do not, you will almost certainly drift and lose momentum and give up before your idea has begun to take shape.

When you're choosing a goal, choose a *big* one for maximum growth. If it's one you have already achieved or can achieve easily, you won't get excited about it. The energy you drive towards the goal will be small, so achieving it won't count as development. You want to choose a goal that really scares you; one that makes you think you are crazy for even attempting it; one that you have no idea how to get. Close friends and family may comment on how ridiculous it is, which is when you know you are on the right path. You'll know in your heart why you want it, but will probably have no idea how to get there. Focus on that goal so your awareness rises. Before long, you will see hints and signs everywhere that you can follow to move in the direction of your goal.

For example, the first step you need to take could be securing finance. When you think of all of the ways you could get the finance you need, the right one will become clear. You may receive a phone call from a friend telling you about an angel investor or venture capitalist they have started to work with and this is exactly what you have been searching for. You ask them for the investor's contact details, set up a meeting and begin your journey towards achieving your goal.

The key to success is awareness. In our example, if you had not been aware that you were looking for support in the area of finance, you would likely have missed this opportunity.

How do you decide what goal you want to achieve? It must be heartfelt, but it may be that you are passionate about many parts of your life like yoga, arts and crafts, science, drawing or helping people. You must choose the one that stands out; the one that you are most passionate about; the hobby that you can turn into a professional business; the one that you can make enough money from. After all, you still need to replace your income and pay your bills.

When you love what you do, you are likely to wonder why earning money was so difficult for you in the past. Be warned: you may go through a period of imposter syndrome when you think someone is going to tap you on the shoulder and call you out as a fake; that you aren't good enough to be doing this type of work. You are not alone in this; it has happened to many successful people.

This feeling slowly subsides as you grow into yourself and gain more confidence. You'll realise you are good enough; you do deserve to be doing what you are doing. When you recognise the negative chatter that holds you back, you'll be able to change the words you say to yourself into positive ones. Your mindset then turns from negative to positive and you gain momentum as you move towards your goal.

Choose a goal that scares you, impress the goal into your subconscious mind by repetition and add to it until it takes shape. Exercising your mind is no different to exercising any other muscle in your body. Be creative. Once you have the complete image in your mind's eye, you will become emotionally attached to the goal and think of it many times throughout the day. This moves it from your conscious mind into your subconscious mind, which is where your feelings are held. The goal is now your heart's desire so you'll feel the pull towards achieving it. This is when you start to take action.

EXERCISE: MEDITATE YOUR WAY TO GOALSETTING CLARITY

If you're stuck on which goal to work on, meditation can often break through to what you really believe in rather than what others think you should achieve. Meditation cuts out the white noise and goes straight to the heart and soul of the matter so your authentic self can impact your logical mind. When you are at one with your spirit in meditation, you are at your most creative and your true wants and desires come to the surface.

You may not be able to decide between two or more goals that you are passionate about. When this happens with my clients, I carry out a deep guided meditation together with them to take them through the visions in their mind from start to finish.

It may be that meditation is already a regular part of your life, or this may be something you can do with a mentor or expert in mindfulness. Either way, it is an excellent way of gaining clarity on what you really want. At the end of the meditation, you immediately write down all your thoughts and desires, giving colour to the picture of each goal in your mind. You can then look with renewed clarity at the processes and resources you will need for each one and what impact each will have on your personal life.

Once you have insight into the fine details of what you want and why you want it, you're likely to feel much lighter within yourself as your internal processes will no longer be in conflict. This clear direction on how to move forward is highly conducive to excitement about getting started in your quest to achieve a goal you know is the right one for you.

Summary

In this chapter, we looked at the questions you need to ask yourself when you're wanting to change, why you want more from life and what you need to do to make those changes. Change is not easy, but if you want to achieve big things, you need to set big goals.

Become both a teacher and a student as you ask for help from those around you and share the experience of success with them. When you come to form a team, choose people who are smarter than you so their skills complement yours and you will always have people to ask for advice and help. It is not a weakness to ask for help, but a true strength of your character. Others then come to understand your why and see your vision.

If you don't tend to make decisions quickly, ask yourself why as this can negatively impact on your forward momentum. Decision making is key to ensuring things happen so when you work towards your goal, you gain momentum quickly.

Do you really need a mentor? The answer is a resounding yes. Having a mentor or mentors is important at every stage of your business journey as they can fast-track you towards your goals. With the right mindset, you may eventually achieve your goal on your own, but a mentor could save you months or even years in the process.

How big should your goal be? A small goal will not satisfy you; strive to achieve a goal that is worthwhile and truly life changing. How do you know the goal is right for you? A good tip is to try meditation. Then your heart will tell you.

PART TWO
CHANGING YOUR MINDSET

3
Understand Yourself

In this chapter, we will build on the answers to the questions we asked ourselves in Chapter 2. We now know our strengths and weaknesses, so we have already begun to build up a story of ourselves, to understand ourselves deeply.

Often, we tell ourselves false tales that we have learned as children. Having repeated these stories over and over in our minds, by the time we grow into adults, we believe they are actual facts. What we need to realise is that they're not our own stories at all, but our parents', siblings', teachers' and peers' beliefs projected on to us. To fully understand ourselves, we must unlearn these stories and replace them with our own thoughts and beliefs.

Understand your passion

When you think about making a living doing what you really enjoy, how does it make you feel? Are you normally too busy doing the things that you need to do to get to the next stage of your business journey to consider these feelings? Are you only focusing on the end goal?

When you notice how you feel while doing the things you are passionate about, you may be surprised at what comes up. At first, there could be a lot of self-doubt, but this will be short lived when you achieve success working on what you enjoy. When you use your skills and passion to help someone solve a problem that they have, a problem that may seem huge to them and cause them a lot of stress, it is a bonus when you get paid for what you do. You'll feel alive within yourself when you are working on your passion and give out an energetic vibe that attracts likeminded people to you. Excited about your work, you'll feel like a child again, full of enthusiasm and dreams. The service you give to others will be repaid to you ten-fold, but maybe not in the way you expect.

Many people look at Karma in the negative sense, regarding it as payback for someone doing a wrong to someone else, but I have experienced Karma in the positive sense in my personal life as well as my business life. There is always a lesson to be learned and I keep encountering the same lesson until I have

UNDERSTAND YOURSELF

learned it, broken the pattern and changed the behaviour, never to repeat it.

Once you have broken a destructive pattern or habit, you're likely to see that it was worth the hard work to learn the lesson. Elation, positive pride and confidence are three of the many benefits I have enjoyed as a result, and you can too. You'll then be able to set higher boundaries for yourself so that you'll no longer tolerate destructive patterns or accept the type of behaviour you may have put up with in the past. These boundaries will be reflected in your friends and clients' changed behaviours towards you. Clients will no longer ask you to do menial tasks for them and you'll be able to reach out to a new level of client.

When you get to this stage, you'll likely receive more business proposals and have the luxury of being able to sift through the opportunities that are presented to you, saying yes only to the ones that are financially viable. You may even get the chance to network with your business idols, people you always dreamed of working with. You'll learn so much from these individuals when you understand their why and see what got them to their point of success. In this personal and professional growth spurt, you may find yourself able to work on many different projects at the same time, all of which fulfil you in different ways.

When you are happy, which you are likely to be when you're spending your life doing things you are passionate about, the people around you will notice and want to know your secret. The truth is, there is no secret; you are simply living your life fulfilled, which is what we are all destined to do. In this state, you will be able to deal with issues that come your way with ease and without drama so they are short lived and don't have a huge impact on your life.

It is a myth that successful or wealthy people don't have problems. On the surface, their lives may seem perfect, but when you look closely, you can see they experience the same problems as everyone else. There is one difference, though: they have studied themselves and others, which allows them to read people quickly. They can then engage and react to a problem from a perspective that allows them to dismiss it in minutes rather than days or weeks as they are keen to move forward as quickly as possible.

When we look at a problem from a place of passion, we can take responsibility for it and strive to resolve it. We won't drag it out, blame others or approach the problem from a negative perspective; we act with a positive mindset and see the problem as an opportunity for growth instead of a roadblock. When we want to grow and have the passion to succeed in anything we choose to do, problems are replaced with solutions.

CASE STUDY: TONY ROBBINS

Tony Robbins is an American philanthropist who studies people to find out what makes them get out of bed in the morning. He then writes books and holds seminars all over the world, teaching individuals and business owners what they need to help them to grow, improve and ultimately become better versions of themselves. Understanding what people feel passionate about, he believes that there is no limit to growth.

Tony meditates every day, which gives him a strong mind. Anyone can have difficult situations to deal with, but by confronting issues head on, he no longer has bad days, but a bad 'few hours'.[9] With a strong why behind him, he has built a career around doing the things he is passionate about. This passion has led to him becoming one of the most inspirational people on the planet.

Understand your vulnerability

When we decide to start our own business, we open ourselves up for others to comment on our personal and professional lives. We receive help in many formats, from the concerned family member who asks us if we are doing the right thing to entrepreneurs who have succeeded before us spurring us on. The former

---

9 E Carmichael, 'What Tony Robbins does every morning (powerful daily ritual)', (2018), www.youtube.com/watch?v=6lFg_Im8Ly0, accessed 18 May 2022

may think they are supporting us when actually they are holding us back; the latter truly believe in us.

Concerned friends and family members may mean well and their comments come from a place of love, but they do not help us. When the people we care about, people who have been our rock for our entire life, are not supportive, it can easily cause us to doubt ourselves. Up until this point, we have probably taken their advice, which may well have turned out to be sound, so we wonder if we are being selfish for turning our back this time. Why do we want more than they have? Doubts that we are not smart enough, not good enough to be a successful businessperson can easily creep in if we're not careful. Who would want to buy from us anyway? When the negative voices in our head drown out the positive ones, before we know it, we may be planning to give up on our dream because it is the easier option.

On the other side of the coin, fellow entrepreneurs become our tribe. They are already running successful companies and seem to have it all, so we need to seek their advice. They tell us the harsh reality of what it takes to succeed so we get a full picture rather than the airy-fairy Instagram stories of a serial entrepreneur who is only interested in popularity. We then know how much hard work we need to do to start our own business, but with a burning desire within us, a strong why, we can do it. Now's the time to decide to move forward.

The concerned family members may still try to discourage us. There will also be the naysayers who want us to fail due to their own insecurities and jealousies. We have our tribe encouraging us to move forward, but we may sometimes feel torn between these two groups. With fire in our belly, we need to decide to succeed. Failing is not an option.

With this decision, our feelings of vulnerability are replaced by an awareness we've likely never had before. We realise that people who love us give us advice based on their own life experiences, not ours. At first, we may feel confused and frustrated because all we want is for them to be on our side, but with the tools and people to support us, we are guided in the right direction and our feelings of vulnerability diminish.

You cannot tell your nearest and dearest you are going to succeed; you can only show them by your results. This means your sales figures, bank balance, successful relationships, happiness and abundance, which prove beyond doubt that you believe in yourself and so does your tribe.

Bear in mind that vulnerability is a useful tool as well. You need to make yourself vulnerable to walk in the footsteps of your clients, going through their pain to understand how to meet their needs. Only when you fully understand what their problem is can you offer the solution.

Think back to a time you had a problem that needed solving and you asked an expert to help you, perhaps a gardener, cleaner, joiner, plumber or electrician. I'm sure you didn't think twice about calling for the support of these experts because you knew they fully understood the problem you needed solving; this is how you want your clients to feel when they call you. If someone has a problem, then there needs to be someone to solve it. Once you have a thorough understanding of the problem, you can provide that solution and get paid for it.

As we move from one growth level to another, we may feel like everyone can see into our soul and feel what we are feeling. This can make us feel incredibly vulnerable as we peel away each layer and highlight our insecurities, but we need to look introspectively into those parts of ourselves that we have kept hidden for years and ask ourselves why we feel these insecurities. Some issues may be more painful than others to work through, but we must address each one head on, squash it and dissolve it. Then we close the gap of vulnerability and shut down the negative talk in our head. We stop caring what others think of us and focus on our goals, looking at our results from yesterday and seeking to improve them. If we need to employ a new member of staff, take a training course or purchase the latest piece of software, we do so to save ourselves time in our business, upskill ourselves personally and improve our services.

When we overcome our insecurities and up our game in this way, the likelihood is others will be watching us with interest, impressed by our results. At this point, we have the experience and skills to give back in the form of volunteering, training or coaching to teach others the importance of knowing who they are so they too can take control of their lives.

Understand why you should compete only with yourself

When we look left and right to see what our competitors are doing, we lose focus on the direction we are moving in. We spread our energy across the board and become distracted, missing opportunities that come our way. Caught up in the drama of what competitors are doing and how they are doing it, we often allow insecurities to build up within ourselves. Are we perhaps not as good as them?

In business, there are no competitors. There is only one of you and no one else can replicate your story. There is no one on this planet who has had the same experiences or followed the same path as you, so they cannot possibly run exactly the same business as you. People buy from people, so if you know who you are and understand what you are selling, you will attract the right people to your business. There may be other businesses in your industry selling what you are selling, but they are not selling it in the same way as you.

It is healthy to keep an eye on what your competitors are doing, but don't let it get out of hand. Instead, concentrate on your business and ask yourself if you would buy your own product or service. The answers may show you the need to make some tough decisions and get rid of dead wood.

A word of warning, though: *do not offer discounts to your clients*. This cheapens you as an individual and devalues your service. Set boundaries with your clients and offer the high level of service you want them to come to expect from you. Then you gain their respect as you show them you are the expert in your field.

When you stay in your own lane and focus on improving yourself and your business, you keep yourself knowledgeable about the most up-to-date legislation. You can hire the best staff on the market, up-level your own skills and stay relevant to what is happening in the world around you. Remain open to change and the possibilities are endless. Observing your own business from the point of view of a client, you can always make the right improvements.

Be kind to those around you as this kindness will be repaid to you in many ways. Listen to your staff and invite them to give their opinion, involving them in achieving your goals and working with them to achieve theirs. Look at every section of your business with your team and take note of where you can make upgrades. When you take action in each of these areas, your business will grow.

Set yourself financial targets and work towards achieving them, making sure your team is onboard to help you. Every business success needs to be a team effort as they benefit too. Keep a positive outlook on your business and life in general and know exactly where you're heading in both. Clear direction and focus will not be diminished by what others are doing and you'll likely be too focused on achieving your goals to notice those of your competitors anyway.

When you do all this, you will attract your ideal client. They will be drawn to your business's values and ethics and become your tribe as they have the same core values as you. They'll want to work with you because they believe in you. Then you can build a level of trust with clients and teams that is imperative to your success, surrounding yourself with likeminded people who want to support you.

This trust will encourage your tribe to tell their friends and family about you. Marketing your business can be cumbersome and time consuming, so word-of-mouth recommendations are like gold dust. Ensure that clients always receive a high level of service to keep that trust going so you and your business are worthy of compliments. People are quick to say what they don't like but seem to find it much harder to say what they *do* like.

Ask for client testimonials and receive any praise you get graciously. By keeping your head down and staying in your own lane, you're likely to end up delighted with how your business will progress in a short space of time. All this without giving a second thought to your competitors.

CASE STUDY: A SUCCESSFUL CHANGE OF MINDSET

A client approached me to mentor him for a business development project. He had a marketable product that could help a lot of people, but although the market was not saturated, there were others doing what he was proposing to do. Unfortunately, he was focusing on these competitors and his energy was becoming diluted. As a result, he was losing momentum in driving his product to market.

I mentioned this to him early in our conversation and he explained in great detail why he felt he needed to observe his competitors. After twenty minutes of letting him talk, I wanted to know one thing: why was he wasting so much time on worrying what other people were doing instead of focusing on developing his own product?

He went quiet for a few minutes, then told me he didn't have an answer for me. That didn't matter; he'd realised he needed to change his way of thinking to one that would serve him. He believed wholeheartedly in his product but was not putting his energy into taking the action needed to get it in front of the relevant people.

That day, he changed his mindset from caring what other people were doing to focusing on how many clients he could help. In doing that, he changed the purpose of his goal to a more rewarding one. He thought creatively on how he would develop his product and applied for a grant from his local university for research and development, which he received with ease. This allowed him to hire staff, buy the best equipment and corresponding software, and pay himself for his time. His product is now gaining traction.

Understand how to build resilience

When we were children, most of us were happy go lucky. Nothing really impacted our life. We were protected by those around us who took charge of the difficult situations that occurred, so we felt safe and loved.

As we moved into our teenage years, we learned that life is not so smooth sailing and we needed to navigate through each emotional issue of growing up as it arose. Carrying on into adulthood, we all have a choice: either deal with each issue head on or ignore it completely. If we ignore it, we may think we have got away with it, but the issue tends to repeat itself throughout our life until we address it. Only at that point do we feel the growth within.

With every issue we address, we build resilience. This makes us stronger on the inside and better equipped to build on this strength. The next time we are faced with a struggle, we feel more comfortable about resolving it as we have developed the tools to find the answers. This is why it is best to face a problem within us head on, learn lessons from it and vow never to repeat the mistake.

For those of us who walk away from an inner problem instead of dealing with it head on, life can feel difficult. We often believe we're unlucky in business, relationships, bringing up children and so on because bad things seem to keep 'happening to' us, but the hard truth is that we have attracted all these bad things into our life. Life is happening *for* us not *to* us.[10]

When we are down on our luck, we tend to think negatively about ourselves and have low self-esteem. This can lead to us feeling sorry for ourselves or never having any money or always being sick. We may moan repeatedly about our illness, our conflicts and the job we detest, if we have a job at all. Our results are negative, and this is directly related to our lack of resilience, which in turn is a result of us not dealing with the problems within.

Are you feeling lost? Do you not feel you have the power within you to make the change and move away from a life that is not serving you well? Once

---

10 beUmore, 'Life is always happening for us not to us – Tony Robbins – Motivation', (2017), www.youtube.com/watch?v=bv8Ox3_6sFY&ab_channel=beUmore, accessed 14 June 2022

you reach rock bottom, there is only one way to go and that is upwards.

If this is where you are, decide right now that you are no longer prepared to accept this life and set yourself small changes to make each day, working towards milestones. Without the resilience you need, you may feel overwhelmed by the amount you have to do to change your life completely, so look for support, ideally from a mentor. You cannot do this quickly; it's an impossible mountain to climb all at once, but when you put one foot in front of the other and break it down into bite-size pieces, it seems more manageable.

Once you've got going, review your progress and reward yourself at each milestone you achieve. Build on the layers of strength, confidence and resilience you gain at each milestone and slowly progress, and then repeat the process. For every action step you take, you will feel more comfortable within yourself and trust your own judgement more.

When you realise what you like and don't like, you can set strong boundaries concerning what you are prepared to accept from other people, and stick to them. You will gain the resilience to take full responsibility for your actions and apologise when you are in the wrong, never blaming others or allowing them to influence your decisions. When your self-respect rises, others will respect you in turn.

When you get good at facing up to problems within and build your resilience further, you can repeat this process in every part of your life, analysing your results and continuously growing. Then you can help others around you to do the same. You'll become a person you are proud to be, a person other people want to be around.

Patience is a key factor in building resilience; it is a slow burn that can take many years. When we decide to make a change to our life, we may be tempted to give up and retreat to our old ways when this change doesn't happen quickly. We may tell ourselves stories, believing we have failed because we did not have the right knowledge, money or support and ignoring what we could have done differently.

This is a reason 20% of businesses fail in their first year.[11] The likelihood is the business owner wasn't born resilient, nor did they learn resilience throughout their life, so they gave up too easily, before they'd even got started. These business owners don't post their hardships on social media, unlike the laptop-lifestyle entrepreneurs, so we don't get to see what they faced. Building a business is hard, make no mistake, which is why resilience is an essential quality.

---

11 T Carter 'The true failure rate of small businesses', *Entrepreneur* (2021), www.entrepreneur.com/article/361350, accessed 18 May 2022

CASE STUDY: AN ENTREPRENEUR'S DREAM FALLS VICTIM TO LACK OF RESILIENCE

A few years ago, an entrepreneur dreamed of opening a coffee shop in her local town. She believed that it would be a great way to socialise with family and friends and make some money in the process, but she went into the business with her eyes closed. She underestimated the costs involved to convert the premises into a working kitchen, as well as paying rent, rates, staff costs and herself.

Unfortunately, this entrepreneur had never looked inside herself to deal with the problems lurking within, so she didn't have the resilience to face the issues head on. She blamed the builders who carried out the conversion for overcharging her, her staff for (allegedly) stealing from the till and the monthly bills for being too high. Working twelve-hour days, she was suffering from exhaustion and was overwhelmed. She required a mentor to help her build her resilience and dive into each of the business issues, but it was another cost she couldn't afford.

Her negative energy was infectious, and customers didn't want to spend long in her coffee shop environment, so she didn't get repeat business. In the end, her sales figure was simply too low to keep the business afloat.

Lacking either support or, more importantly, inner resilience, this entrepreneur became stressed and within twelve months, she closed the doors of her business for the last time. With the right tools, mentoring and resilience, hers – like any business – could have been a success.

Understand why you should act on your goals

You may have heard people say that your thoughts become your reality, but many people do not believe this to be true. Instead, they believe that life is a series of events that are not linked to each other and happen to them instead of for them. In fact, we can all control our lives by converting our thoughts into reality.

For successful entrepreneurs, this is especially true; in fact, it is key to their business. They schedule hours or even days into their diary for thinking, creating a set of goals that can take their business to the next level.

As an entrepreneur, you are likely to be working on many goals at one time. Some goals are bigger than others and take longer to materialise; some you will discard after a second glance. Pinpoint the goals that achieve the biggest growth and plan on how to move towards each one, visualising them in your mind many times to refine each minute detail until the picture is clear. Once you can see your goal in your mind's eye as clearly as if it were real, you can tell others exactly what it looks like. Use your higher mental faculties such as your imagination to create the goal.

Goal setting makes us feel good. We all want to be successful for ourselves and the ones we love, and goals help us not only to get material items, but also to grow as we work towards them. This growth allows us to improve in every area of our life, not just our business.

EXERCISE: HOW THOUGHTS BECOME YOUR REALITY

This exercise is designed to help you to visualise the person you need to be to accomplish the things you want in life.

First, identify a goal that is aligned with your personal values. It could be a professional aim, for example, to increase your income to six figures in a twelve-month period, or something personal, for example, to give up eating meat or be in a healthy relationship where both parties' needs are met.

Write about the desires linked to the goal in a lot of detail: envisage who you will be and how you will feel once you've achieved it.

Now, reverse engineer yourselves from that version of yourself back to who you are today by writing out the steps you need to take to become the person that has already achieved that goal. Examples could be making contact with someone who is already working in a particular field, looking for office premises, creating a website, applying for a bank loan, researching therapists or signing up for an evening course.

Looking at your goals in terms of 'future you' will help you to see what work you need to do on yourself to become that person.

Summary

In this chapter, we have looked at how to understand ourselves, deeply and honestly. We have looked at our passion, vulnerability, competing only with ourselves, building resilience and how to organise our thoughts into goals that remain true to our values.

Being passionate about anything we do in life gives us a sense of purpose, a reason to get out of bed in the morning. When we talk about what we are passionate about, our eyes light up and we could go on for hours. Our energy draws people towards us.

To be honest about what makes us happy, we must allow ourselves to be vulnerable, which can be a scary place. Vulnerability has a positive side too, though: it enables us to put ourselves in our customers' shoes, understand their pain points and come up with the perfect solution to solve them.

When we have opened ourselves to our vulnerability and discovered who we truly are, we won't need to look to others for support as much, as everything we need will be within us. This is when we find it easy to stop comparing ourselves to other people and concentrate on growing our own business. We are all only in competition with ourselves as no one else can be us, nor can we be them.

UNDERSTAND YOURSELF

We can regard every knockback we receive in life as a blessing, using it as an opportunity to learn and build our resilience. The more resilience we build, the more equipped we will be not only to cope with setbacks in the future, but to grow from them.

When we as entrepreneurs set time aside to think and use our imagination, we can pinpoint the inner thoughts that are important to our development and organise them into goals. Goals, of course, bring us closer to our heart's desire, allowing us to improve in every aspect of our life.

4
Align

In this chapter, we will bring together everything we have covered so far and see how it all aligns with our core values. We now know what beliefs are truly ours and which are other people's beliefs projected on to us. Looking deeply inside ourselves, we have gained a full understanding of our strengths, our goals and our desires.

When everything we do aligns with our values, we can fully accept and love ourselves, and this is when the magic truly happens. We will be so focused and strong that we will easily be able to convert our hopes and dreams into reality. Our energy will be potent and positive, empowering us from within.

Align with gratitude

While many people believe gratitude just means saying thank you for something we've received, it is actually more than that. We need to be grateful for everything we have in our life right now, from material items like a home or a car to having people we can rely on. These are the people who fully support us in whatever we do, even if they don't agree with us.

As entrepreneurs who want to grow, we need to set goals that others may think ridiculous, outside of our knowledge base or unachievable in our lifetime. Only we have the vision to see the outcome clearly before it has happened, so to begin with at least, it is best to keep the big goals between ourselves and our mentor. When we know we are fully aligned with our goal and nothing can stop us, those who trust us will support us and know we will achieve the desired outcome. They will encourage us, believe in us and help us when we are stuck. Isn't that something well worth showing gratitude for?

Imagine waking up in the morning feeling low on energy. Maybe you have a head cold, maybe you're just not feeling good about yourself. When you look in the mirror and see your tired reflection, it can be easy to listen to the negative chatter in your head, telling you you're too sickly or too old to strive for your goals. Leaving the bathroom, perhaps you stub your toe. Maybe you go to make a cup of tea to find there's no milk.

After this bad start, you're likely to find your day continues in a negative way and you feel like the world is against you. Why did you bother to get out of bed in the first place? If you allow it to, this pattern can easily repeat itself over days, weeks and months; before you realise it, you are on a downward spiral that seems impossible to break away from. You cannot achieve anything good with this type of mindset, so you need to put a stop to it. But how exactly do you pick yourself up?

A better way to start your day every morning is to check in with yourself to see how you are feeling. This gives you a reference point as to how you are right now compared to where *you* want to be, not where others believe you ought to be. There is a whole day ahead of you in which to make great things happen, so take a deep breath and ask yourself from a position of gratitude how you are feeling.

EXERCISE: MEL ROBBINS'S 5 SECOND RULE

Author and motivational speaker Mel Robbins devised the 5 second rule. The principle behind this rule is simple: do not engage your brain before you make a decision, so that you can truly follow your heart. She believes if you allow your thoughts time to take shape, they can affect your mind and trick you into not doing something that could be potentially good for you.

> For example, when your alarm clock goes off, jump out of bed within five seconds before any negative thoughts kick in. In her book *The 5 Second Rule*,[12] Mel tells us she used this concept when she was going through a particularly bad patch in her life as a coping technique. Rather than lying in bed feeling sorry for herself and not making any changes to the situation, she would get up right away and face the day with gratitude for everything that was positive in her life. Now she speaks all over the world about the 5 second rule because she has such belief in the impact it can make to everyone's lives.

If you wake up sluggish, you have the choice to change what you are feeling by using the 5 second rule coupled with gratitude to your advantage. Add the ritual of daily gratitude into your morning routine to guarantee you start your day on the right footing.

Write a list of ten things that you are grateful for now and ten things you want to happen in the future, wording all twenty in the present tense. This will help you to look at and appreciate everything you have in your life today, becoming aware that even the smallest things can give you a sense of safety. You are worthy of nice things; you are a good person; and you do deserve what others have.

---

[12] M Robbins *The 5 Second Rule: Transform your life, work, and confidence with everyday courage* (Post Hill Press, 2017)

Every day that you practise gratitude, build on the day before. You are likely to find you will soon stop looking at others in envy and feel better about yourself, and your confidence will naturally grow. Once you have repeated your daily gratitude ritual every day for at least a week, it'll become a natural part of your morning routine and you'll do it without thinking.

Notice how you feel before and after you practise your morning gratitude; you're likely to spot a profound difference. For my part, after practising gratitude, my energy is higher, I feel lighter within myself, my mood has lifted and I'm motivated to carry out my daily tasks.

When you feel positive within yourself, you can see challenges as opportunities rather than obstacles and take them on more easily. You can work through problems and review them once you've resolved them to understand what you've learned. This is part of your growth.

Daily gratitude shifts our vibration, uplifts our energy and has a direct impact on our mood, but many people underestimate its power. They do not connect the dots that the physical act of writing out ten things in their lives to be grateful for can impact on their emotional state.

Being grateful for the things and people in our life is a form of self-care. Many of us are quick to lift others up but forget that we are also important. We have needs to be met. Being grateful is about being kind to ourselves and putting ourselves first, which is vitally important. If we are not kind to ourselves, we deplete our reserves of energy and leave ourselves in no position to help others. This is the reason the pilot on a plane tells us to put our oxygen mask on first in the event of an emergency. If we do not fill ourselves up with everything we need, we cannot help others.

Having a positive mindset is key to living our best life because when problems arise, we have a choice in how to handle them. If we see a solution, we can move away from the problem so its negative energy diminishes. People with a negative mindset tend to discuss, ponder and procrastinate over a problem, which can then gain momentum and grow. The phrase 'adding fuel to the fire' describes perfectly what we do when we're facing a problem in a negative mindset. A great way to make sure we face every day and any problems it brings with a positive mindset is to start the day by practising gratitude.

Align your thoughts

We meet successful people in business, and we meet just as many unsuccessful people. Is there is a link between success and thoughts?

As business owners, we all have ideas that start as small thoughts. We take these thoughts and add details to give them shape and momentum. Then we build on the thoughts more and more until they become imprinted on our mind and feel as real as something we can touch. This is when we believe that our seed of an idea could become real one day.

Initially, it's best to act on one thought, one idea at a time, maybe setting up a meeting with someone who can help us, interviewing potential members of staff who see our vision in the same way that we do or viewing an office or warehouse where we could produce our products or meet our clients. In time, we take the idea, which was once just a thought, and turn it into reality in the form of a product or service that solves a problem for our ideal client. We can then start making money from it.

This doesn't just work in business, but in any part of life. Think back to a dream holiday, car or home. If it was something truly aligned to your inner desires, you're likely to have wanted it so badly, you thought about it every day. Nothing or no one would stop you from having it. Even if you had to save like you had never saved before, you got the money together to make the final payment.

Positivity or negatively will bring you more of the same. Depending on your perspective, how you decide to look at a situation, whether your glass is half full or half empty, you will attract positive or negative energy into your life. The good news is that you get to choose. You decide whether to accept positivity or negativity. This awareness allows you to choose what you want more of, such as a business you are passionate about, and what you want to remove from your life, such as negative people or a job you hate. There are no limitations to what you can achieve; the only prerequisite is that you align your goals with your heart's desire and pursue your passion in life.

The most successful entrepreneurs understand the importance of the creative process to levelling up their business. Without creativity, their business will become stagnant, flatline and eventually decline. Any business owner who does not stay current and on top of their game will lose sales. It is important to keep a business moving forward, attend training courses and improve the soft skills which can be equally as important as the main income stream.

Once you're up and running, allocate thinking time in your business as part of the working week to make sure your ideas and passion are aligned. This practice isn't just for the millionaires of this world; it is for you too. Many business owners have their best ideas during this process. This is so important that it is the subject of the exercise at the end of this chapter.

During your thinking time, create several ideas, then later discard the ones that don't align with your passion and values and act on the others. This process allows you to work on many goals at one time. Some will be short-term goals that can be obtained in a matter of months while others can take a year or more. Thanks to the generating of ideas that you do in your thinking time, you can achieve most of the smaller goals without giving them much focus, freeing you up to pay all your attention to the long-term goal.

Align with your intuition

You need to use your intuition when making decisions or working towards your goal to ensure you are on the right path. Check in with yourself regularly so you don't move off that path and head in the wrong direction.

You may well have heard people talking about listening to their gut. You may also have heard them complain that when they did not, it led to situations that they later regretted. Our 'gut' is our intuition, an inbuilt system designed to keep us from danger.

Intuition comes from the days many millennia ago when humans had to make split-second decisions that would literally save their lives, and it's still serving us well – as long as we listen to it. It is our immediate understanding of whether someone or something is good or bad for us. This initial reaction on an emotional level comes from our subconscious mind. We often don't know on a conscious level until sometime in the future what the understanding was that our subconscious came to, but it is always the right decision.

In all aspects of life, we will get the best results when we are aligned with our gut. Our beliefs and core values are linked to our gut, which is why we feel uneasy and uncomfortable within ourselves when we don't follow our intuition. We have an urge to course correct immediately. When we deal with this feeling of unease head on and change course so we are following our gut, we tend to feel like a weight has been lifted off us; that we are back on the track we should have been on in the first place.

If you take a wrong turn, don't dwell on your misdirection. Simply take it as a lesson to trust your gut the next time it tells you how to deal with a situation.

Not everyone is aware of their intuition so, of course, they cannot respond to it. Intuition acts like a muscle: it requires constant use to increase its function, its 'muscle memory', and allow you to react instinctively to the feelings you get. This instinctive feeling sends a signal to your brain to move away from danger, for example not to work with a certain individual or on a certain goal. You have a choice to accept or reject this feeling; remember, though, that your gut is aligned with your core values and keeps you on target.

In business and life, people will always give you their opinion whether you ask for it or not. When you are certain the decisions you make are aligned with your values, other people's opinion becomes irrelevant to you, so you can thank them politely for their advice and continue on your own path. Their thoughts may be right for their gut, but they are not right for yours. Often, these people love you dearly and do not want you to fail, but if they really had your best interests at heart, they would ask you how you feel about the situation and if you have any concerns. They would trust your judgement that you know what you are doing, and what you don't know, you and your mentor will find out.

When you listen to your heart, you can never go wrong in life. If you are ego led and follow your head over your heart, you're likely to act in a way that is somewhat transactional, which can come across as one-sided and selfish. You may seem arrogant and uncaring about what others think, perhaps even putting others in danger. Think of the hardnosed businessperson who tramples over others in their team to get to the top. They do not work in alignment with their core values, so they cheat as many people as possible and pay as little tax as they can get away with. I'm sure that's not a person you aspire to be.

When you act in alignment with your gut, you'll have a much more favourable outcome, often helping others along your way to success without even being aware of this. You will be paid back in droves for this help as you will end up with a huge network of like-minded people ready to support you at any time.

CASE STUDY: INTUITION SAVES A CLIENT FROM A COSTLY MISTAKE

A client wanted to discuss a business opportunity that had been presented to him. He had been approached by a business owner who wanted to exit their company and had invited my client to purchase it. The company was in the same industry as my client's business, so his relevant knowledge was high and the overall risk was low.

My client came to me for advice on whether to move forward with this business venture. He knew it would give him exponential growth, but something was holding him back. We looked closely at the figures and realised it was a viable business with a good reputation, a well-known brand and a high-value client base that stretched across a number of local towns and villages. The bank had agreed to provide the finance and everything was set to move forward, but something was niggling at my client. Something didn't feel right.

My client felt something was awry with the business owner. He had a feeling that the owner was withholding information, but he didn't have any proof or evidence to back up what he was feeling. His gut was telling him to watch out for something that he couldn't see for himself with his logical mind.

Instead of rushing ahead and closing the deal, he decided to take a few days to review everything before making his final decision. After some time, he decided not to enter into the deal. Many people voiced their opinion that he should have moved forward and had missed out on a unique opportunity, but he stuck to his decision and trusted it was the correct one for him.

He later found out via the grapevine that a competitor had purchased the company. Everything seemed to be working well until almost a year later when the company went into liquidation at great cost to the purchaser. This was shocking news to all in the industry as it was such an unusual thing to happen.

It transpired that the owner had been stealing from the company and, of course, had not disclosed this. My client believed that he would have ended up in the same situation as his competitor had he proceeded with the deal and was relieved he had listened to his intuition.

Align your self-esteem and confidence

Our self-esteem and confidence are directly linked to our success. The type of client we attract matches our level of confidence in ourselves.

When we start out in business, we tend to have a handful of clients who require our full attention. They take up all our time, but the likelihood is we do not charge anywhere near as much as we should because we are keen to help them solve their problems and build a good reputation within our industry.

A few years into our business, we have more experience as we have been faced with different problems to solve. Our confidence grows and so does our self-esteem, and we value ourselves more. This means we attract a higher-value client who sees us as the expert in our field. We can then focus on being the best version of ourselves, up-levelling our skills at every opportunity. We set new boundaries with ourselves, our staff and our clients.

We cannot manage our time, but we can manage our activities. With our confidence and self-esteem high, we stop carrying out activities that are outside the scope of our engagement contract with clients. In other words, we stop working for free and charge clients for the additional products and services that they request from us, always informing clients of the upgrades we are making to avoid any conflict or confusion in the future.

Clients tend to appreciate this clear picture of the relationship between us. Some may drop off at this point and this is OK; we matched their expectations when we worked with them, but we no longer serve each other. By increasing our self-esteem, we have raised our boundaries and from now on will only attract high-value clients.

This brings up a potential elephant in the room: what should you charge for your services? There is no definitive answer as what you charge varies hugely depending on how you feel about yourself. When you are low in confidence, you're not likely to feel worthy of earning much money so charge a low fee for a high level of service. Even if you have dedicated years to training, kept up to date with the ever-changing market and gained all the certifications you need to carry out your business, you're unlikely to reflect this in what you charge when you have low self-esteem.

Are you so focused on worrying that your clients will shop elsewhere that you keep your prices low? Do you believe low prices will attract your ideal client? This is not the case. You may keep the clients you already have, but they will almost certainly ask for multiple additional services that they are not willing to pay extra for. The work needs to be completed so, if you have set high standards for yourself and your business and aligned them with your values, you will want to complete a task fully and do the extra work for free.

The outcome of this is a downward spiral. Your client loses respect for you and demands more and more. In turn, you're likely to end up getting frustrated with them and the relationship breaks down. In other words, the thing you feared in the first instance – losing your client – has happened.

Focus on offering a high level of products or services to your client. Become the best in your industry, gain the most knowledge and stay at the top of your game.

High confidence and self-esteem will naturally follow. This is when you will attract your ideal clients, the ones aligned with your core values, and you can charge what your skills deserve. Price is no longer an issue to a client who receives a high level of service from a provider they feel aligned with. You can charge what your products and services are worth because your clients see the value you offer them.

You may have multiple clients who pay a high fee for your services and products. You may have a few clients who pay you a huge fee, giving you more time to work on your other income streams. When you repeat this process with all your income streams, the overall outcome is more sales and more money in your bank account. You can reinvest the money you earn into your business to hire quality staff or for research and development, or you may donate some to a charity of your choice, giving back to those in need. Helping others will always bring more meaning and purpose to your life than simply buying material items that are only for show.

You may have heard the phrase 'fake it till you make it' and you may have met people doing exactly that. At first glance, they seem to know what they are talking about as they promise you this and that, but their actions do not match their words.

Consider how you feel when you pay for products or services that you don't receive, or you receive something vastly inferior to what you expected. You're likely to become frustrated. What happens if you raise your concern and receive an apology from the provider, but nothing changes? It won't take long for you to realise the person you are dealing with is not authentic. They are not coming from a place of empathy to solve your problem. They are not good at what they do; they are certainly not the expert they told you they were.

The reason this fake individual fails to meet your expectations is because their self-confidence is extremely low. It was mere bravado that carried them through your initial meeting. Their showmanship drew you in and made you believe in them.

I'm sure this is not how you want to behave in business, nor do you want to work with people who are fakes. Make sure your clients feel how genuine and authentic you are; show that your actions are aligned with your words. When you have high confidence and strong self-esteem, you show a level of certainty which is genuine to the core. Your clients pick up on this when they meet you and will want to work with you and tell their friends about you. These are the best clients you can work with because they are already on your wavelength and aligned with your values.

EXERCISE: BRAIN DUMP

Before we move on from this fascinating topic of alignment and how it can serve you in all walks of life, let's revisit a concept I have touched upon before: the brain dump. Now it's time to take action on aligning your goals and your values.

Grab your diary or open it up on your digital device and schedule in some time in your working week for thinking. Schedule it for as soon as possible, this week if you can. Then block off some time in each working week going forward to the end of the year. It doesn't have to be long, but I would suggest you dedicate at least an hour a week to thinking and planning for yourself and your business. Where possible, schedule this in for the same time each week, then your subconscious will start to work on the problem in the background.

You will be rewarded with a wealth of goals that are aligned with your heart's desire.

During your thinking time, write down as many ideas as pop into your head. It doesn't matter how big, small, crazy they seem; brain dump every last one. Get them out of your head and on to paper or a digital document. Then at a later date, perhaps during your next thinking session, come back to these ideas. The distance you have put between them and you by brain dumping them will help your mind to recognise the ones you really want to pursue and the ones that were just crazy notions after all. Some will excite you, so they're the keepers. Some won't inspire you at all, so bin them.

Now you have the seeds of goals that are truly aligned with you and your business's values. I can't think of many more worthwhile uses of your work time.

Summary

In this chapter, we looked at the importance of aligning everything you do with your core values. When you do this, you will be genuine and authentic and clients will recognise this. You will help others effortlessly and solve their problems, and you will attract your ideal high-value clients.

Gratitude is a hugely beneficial addition to your morning routine. It can direct your energy on a daily basis towards your purpose and your heart's desire. When you follow your gut and practise gratitude, you align your beliefs and actions, and all your strength and focus is directed towards your goal.

It is imperative that you listen to your gut, your intuition, as only by doing this can you pursue goals that are truly aligned to your values. This enables you to trust in yourself, which gives you the confidence to make better decisions and attract the clients you really want to work with.

5
Results

In this chapter, we will see how to use all the skills we have learned to change our results, both in business and in life. We'll look at the initial conversation with clients in which mutual trust is born, how grouping activities saves us time and how focusing on a particular topic sends our energy in that direction. We will learn why a growth mindset is essential for recognising the opportunities to enhance our results and how abundance is so important for our health, wealth and happiness.

The more energy we put towards our goal when we're taking action on it, the more quickly we will achieve it. Once we have achieved a goal, we can complete the Wheel of Life again and compare the two figures, seeing how far we have come and how much we have changed and grown throughout the process. Not only is this an uplifting exercise, it will also show us areas where we still need to increase our focus.

Service

As consumers, we all like to receive a high level of service. When someone goes above and beyond our expectations, we are impressed and grateful for the service we receive. We have the option to give a positive review or contact the business owner directly to give them feedback. If the service is exceptional, we're likely not only to give the business repeat custom, but to recommend it to family and friends whose needs it can meet.

Equally, when we have overpaid for bad service, when we feel that we have been short-changed, we are likely to tell as many people as will listen. We tell the business owner because we want them to improve their services for the future and we may want some form of compensation. We warn people we know not to deal with that business until after the issues have been resolved.

Unfortunately, human nature dictates that not everyone will praise what we do right, but they'll likely jump on our back the moment we get something wrong. This is why consistency is key when we set high standards for our business.

RESULTS

A high level of service can come with its drawbacks. Take a restaurant, for example. You have an excellent meal, the waiting staff are friendly and efficient, the place is clean and airy and the atmosphere welcoming. You enjoy a unique customer experience and are made to feel like the most important person in the restaurant. I'd guess you're highly likely to return to that place in the future.

What happens if you continue to go to that restaurant, having set your expectations so high, and the next time the standard isn't as good? Maybe the waiting staff aren't quite so cheerful; maybe the ambience is missing; maybe the food is slightly cold. The standard is probably far higher than other restaurants in the town, but you're likely to be disappointed.

When we have an image in our mind of what we want, we become frustrated when this is misunderstood by service providers. This is shown time and time again on TV makeover shows or home-interior programmes when the expert completely misinterprets the client's wants and produces something that is in accordance with their own image, not the client's image. This is terribly frustrating for both parties.

The good news is that you can avoid this frustrating situation with your ideal clients. When you initially meet with your client, you have an in-depth conversation. They explain their pain points to you and ask you to solve the problem for them. You explain to them exactly which services you offer that will solve their problem, what each one will cost and the time it will take. You can then agree on a full plan from start to finish.

This conversation can seem difficult because you need to guide them in the right direction, which is not always what they want to hear. They'll have their own image of what they want, but when you explain the facts to them, you leave no room for false expectations. Clients tend to react well to this because they don't want to be surprised with a large bill or an additional service you did not tell them about.

They also want confidence that you have identified their pain point and know exactly how to solve it. By navigating through their worries and answering all their questions during this conversation, explaining that there may be unforeseeable problems arising during the work that you will have to charge more for, you are gaining their trust that you will do what you say you will do.

Your next step is to get to work and act on your promises. If an unexpected issue arises, inform the client immediately, especially where extra fees are concerned. If you make a mistake, apologise as soon as you discover it. Never hide it because the client will ultimately discover it later down the line. It takes courage to do this; it's only natural not to want to admit to making mistakes when someone has come to you because you're an expert in your field, but the trust you have built up with your client will mean they'll be confident you can rectify the issue. In fact, your honesty in owning your mistake is likely to enhance that trust.

When your client trusts you, they will feel a special bond between you; they'll feel supported. You can charge higher fees for your services, which your client is happy to pay as they see their problems solved. They are forever grateful and refer likeminded clients to you who appreciate your services just as much. The word-of-mouth recommendation is a result that benefits every business.

Work smarter, not harder

You may have been told by your parents, family and friends that if you work hard your whole life, you will be successful. If you follow this advice, eventually you'll end up exhausted, juggling work, family and social activities. The immense pressure to keep your house clean, cook meals from scratch, live a healthy lifestyle, look your best and be supportive to everyone around you while growing and improving yourself to keep up in a fast-moving world becomes overwhelming and unrealistic.

It is impossible to be all things to all people. When you are juggling too many balls at the same time, you are inevitably going to drop one at some point. You may feel like your life is spinning out of control and you don't know how to stop it.

The key, as the saying goes, is to work smarter rather than harder. We may not be able to manage our time, but we can manage our activities.

When we have a mountain of activities to get through in one day, sometimes we feel so overwhelmed, we don't know where to start so we end up doing nothing at all. We procrastinate and do menial tasks to avoid facing the problem face on.

To solve the problem of daily activities taking up all of our time, we need to group together similar activities that we can do as a batch. We then need to be confident and decisive in our approach to completing the grouped tasks. Take clearing out a wardrobe at the same time as tidying the bedroom as an example. There is no point in trying on every item in the wardrobe to see if it still fits. Instead, we need to make two piles: one for keeping and one for ditching.

Delegation of tasks can be life changing in your everyday life. Get other people to help with cleaning, emptying the dishwasher and putting away clothes. For the tasks you really dislike, consider hiring help to buy you some time. You can use the time that you save to focus on your business, thereby finding ways to make money that will more than cover the cost of the help.

In your business, you can consider passing more tasks to your support staff; outsourcing or offshoring your product or service; or hiring a virtual assistant to help with your day-to-day admin, reply to emails and set up your booking system for meetings. You can go further and subcontract out your payroll and accountancy services, social media and website scheduling. This frees up your time and energy, allowing you to provide a high level of service to your clients.

The effect grouping and outsourcing activities has on your life is massive. You'll replace overwhelm with patience, stress with calm and gain a new sense of peace. This can only lead to you becoming a nicer person to be around and attracting good things to you.

Focus

To achieve our desired outcome, we must direct our energy in the direction of our dream. When we want something, we need to think about it, visualise it every day until we receive it. Even if we have to work for a few months to save up for it, eventually we will get there if we focus our energy into doing all it takes to achieve our goal.

Children are the best examples of directing their energy towards what they want. They see a toy or a treat and they ask if they can have it. They are relentless in their asking until the parents cannot bear it anymore and either put a stop to it or give in and buy the treat.

When we become adults, we lose this desire and stop wanting so much for ourselves, usually because we were told something like '"I want" never gets' when we were children. We stop using our imagination and dreaming, but the good news is that this is still within us, and we can relearn how to focus on our hopes and desires and unlearn the barriers that have been ingrained in us.

When we have decided what we want to work towards and aligned our goal with our inner values, we must be relentless, like the child in pursuit of that goal. We want to focus all our energy into taking our idea and turning it into a reality. As the goal takes shape in our mind, we become aware of the actions we need to bring it to fruition.

To start with, we may feel like nothing is happening, then we feel a little bit of movement. As we add more people into the mix or set up more meetings or view more business properties, we gain momentum, and after some time has passed, the project seems to be moving by itself. It may even be moving too fast.

Think of it as being like when your car has a flat battery and you need to get out and push it. To start with, the car feels heavy, almost impossible to move. Then suddenly, the tension between the tyres and the road breaks, and the car moves forward. Before long, you have enough momentum to jump-start the car. The engine turns over and the car moves of its own accord.

When you are working with an idea that doesn't excite you, you won't direct enough energy towards making it happen. The lack of excitement could be because it doesn't sit well with your core values or you have already achieved the same goal in the past, so you know you can do it again and don't need to push yourself. Alternatively, you may feel overwhelmed by the amount of work that you need to do to achieve the goal and not know where to start, so instead you do nothing.

If your goal doesn't excite you, the likelihood is you have chosen a safe option, one that doesn't scare you either. You do not have to make any life changes for the goal, so it won't give you much room for growth. It is undesirable and not in line with your life's purpose, so you're likely to give up when you don't get anywhere. What you were doing before seems much easier and less work than carrying on with this boring goal, but if you keep choosing goals that don't stretch you, you're setting yourself up for regret in the future for not pursuing your goal.

Resilience and determination are key factors to sticking to what you believe in to make changes in your life. Nothing comes easily and no one will help you until you reach out and ask for support. No one has ever achieved anything worthwhile without putting their blood, sweat and tears into it. Pure grit and determination are the way to achieve great things. Only you can create your desired life.

CASE STUDY: END-OF-LIFE REGRETS

Some fascinating research was carried out by palliative care nurses looking after patients at the end of their lives.[13] These nurses interviewed patients, asking them many questions about their lives.

One question was related to regrets. The patients were asked if they had any regrets and, if so, what did they regret? The results were astounding.

The fifth most common regret the people on their deathbeds had was a wish that they'd allowed themselves more room to be happy. Number four was a regret at not having stayed in touch with friends, three was sadness at not having had the courage to express their feelings, number two was a wish they hadn't worked so hard. Especially relevant to focusing on what we really want in life, though, is the number-one regret these people had in their dying days: they wished they'd had the courage to live their authentic life rather than trying to please the people around them.

---

13 B Ware 'Regrets of the dying' (Bronnie Ware Blog), https://bronnieware.com/blog/regrets-of-the-dying, accessed 18 May 2022

People often say that others held them back, which is why they didn't follow their dream. The truth is far more likely to be they themselves were too scared to follow their heart for fear of failure. When their health fails and choices are taken from them, they have regrets and dream of the life they could have had if they'd only been brave enough to follow their dreams. Focus your energies on your heart's desire and make sure you don't end up with these regrets.

Growth mindset

When our mind is closed, we tend to miss opportunities that come our way because we are not even aware that they are opportunities. Maybe we get given a rare opportunity to meet an influential person like an angel investor or venture capitalist who could have helped us on our journey, if only we'd realised that we needed that help. Perhaps we miss out on our dream home or trip of a lifetime because we have got so used to saying no to trying new things. We refuse to take on board advice from mentors who wish to steer us in the right direction and shut people who have our best interests at heart out of our lives. We ignore different perspectives on a problem and just believe it's unsolvable.

When we see life through a different lens, through a growth mindset, our results can improve beyond recognition. We say yes to every opportunity that comes our way, even if it scares us. In fact, *especially* if it scares us. We learn about ourselves, our likes and dislikes, what we are good at and what we are not. We mix with likeminded people and build up a tribe of supportive individuals who have our back.

The positive results of a growth mindset are many. Our life has colour and meaning. We wake up excited about the day ahead and believe we will make good things happen. We see opportunities and act on them. It's almost like taking part in a treasure hunt where one clue leads to the next and, ultimately, our desired goal.

CASE STUDY: FROM NO TO YES

The movie *Yes Man* starring Jim Carrey is a perfect illustration of what happens when we say yes to opportunities. At the start of the movie, Carrey's character says no to every opportunity that comes his way. He is depressed, dislikes his job and feels like he has no future. Lacking in energy, he doesn't want to engage in life's opportunities.

Then he meets someone at a conference who challenges him to turn his no into a yes. He decides to take on the challenge because he feels he has nothing else to lose. In the months that follow, he freefalls from a building, learns to speak Korean and takes flying lessons. His life is now fun and has flare. By saying yes to the opportunities that come his way, he is saying yes to life. He is glad that he made such a drastic change because he's received fantastic results that he will be ever grateful for.

Abundance

According to the *Oxford Dictionary of English*, one of the meanings of abundance is 'plentifulness of the good things of life; prosperity'.[14] Some people take this to mean material riches, but that is not necessarily so.

While money provides us with a comfortable lifestyle and is one of the results of business success, I understand abundance to have a deeper meaning: fulfilment within our soul. It means we are living our purpose. We look at every part of our life in separate segments – from our family to our personal relationships to our work – and see how they cross over and interact with each other. We review each segment continuously to add focus to those areas that have become depleted. This brings our life back into balance so we feel happy and content.

Without abundance in our life, our heart is sad and we feel empty inside. Every part of life is a struggle, and we feel we are failing in all areas. This can impact on our self-care, our self-respect and even our health.

---

14 *Oxford Dictionary of English* (Oxford University Press, third edition, 2010)

Overwhelmed and lost, we believe every area of our life is rolled into one mass of chaos that we cannot separate into individual parts.

If this resonates with you, if you are at this point in life, stop whatever you're doing and take a deep breath. You're not alone; there's always a friend or mentor you can ask for help to do some self-healing, but you need to have an awareness that you are feeling this way before you can find a solution.

EXERCISE: TRAVEL FROM PAIN TO ABUNDANCE

A good way to start on your journey back to abundance is by sorting your issues into groups such as family, friends, work, relationships, money. List the problems in each section, placing the biggest issue first, then set about making a plan to work through each of those issues. As with goals, you can always break the solution to the bigger issues down into bite-size pieces and work on them alongside the solutions to the smaller problems.

Maybe you will need to talk to a counsellor, take a course on self-healing or set time aside for some self-care. I recommend you work with a mentor who will check in with your progress at each stage to ensure you do not waver off course.

Make sure each stage of your plan is detailed. Describe your feelings at the start and how you want to feel at the end. At each milestone, have a mini celebration to mark your progress.

This process is not a quick fix by any means and can take months or even years to complete. When you look at every part of your life and decide what changes you are willing to make, you may feel emotional and want to give up, but push through the pain barrier. The results will be worth it.

Summary

In this chapter, we have looked at the positive results we get when we open our mind, spot and act on the opportunities that come our way, and focus on our goals. We looked at how giving the best service possible to our clients while managing their expectations so there are no nasty surprises for them will result in our ideal client being drawn to us. We examined how to group tasks together and outsource them where we can to free up time for us to work on improving ourselves and our business, or simply relax with friends and family. We saw how focusing our energy towards a goal means it gains momentum and speeds us towards our desired results, and how a growth mindset helps us spot those all-important opportunities. Finally, we recognised how essential abundance is to our lives – not just material wealth, but deep fulfilment.

Help is always there if you look for it, and the results of seeking and asking for that help can improve your life beyond recognition.

PART THREE
IMAGINATION MADE REAL

6
Entrepreneur

When we change how we see things, when we look at them with a growth mindset, when we practise daily gratitude, our awareness levels increase and our reaction to certain situations is calmer. We become more patient and see obstacles in life and business as the potential to be creative. We are now thinking as an entrepreneur rather than listening to the negative voice in our head. This is empowering.

With an entrepreneurial mindset, we are well equipped to help others move away from their negative environments. We can teach them the tools to change their life. We are also well equipped to offer services and products to our ideal client that truly solve their problems.

Value pricing

What to charge for a product or service varies between industries and depends on how much in demand your offer is. Apple products and PlayStation consoles, for example, are smartly marketed: only a few hundred are produced at a time to create a frenzy among consumers desperate to own the first models. These companies can set the price point as high as they want because they know that people will pay it.

When you decide how to price your products or services, choose a rate that is in line with your knowledge and experience. If it's a service you offer, price each job dependant on the level and standard of the work you have to put in rather than the time it will take to complete it. If the job may take longer than planned, factor this into your pricing model so you can never end up working for free. When you deliver products or services of a consistently high standard, your clients will value you and have no issue paying your fee.

Make it clear to your client from the outset that you will charge for extra services outside the remit of your engagement. If something arises that you had not picked up on initially, especially if it will cause the job to take significantly longer and cost more than you'd expected, tell your client before you start this extra work. The worst thing you can do is say nothing and present your client at the end of the job with a larger bill than they had anticipated or budgeted for.

Show you're transparently honest right from the start to gain your client's trust and avoid awkward conversations from arising in the future.

Using this pricing model, you don't set a limit on what you can earn in a year. If you charge by the hour, there are only a certain number of hours in the day that you can allocate to chargeable work. The rest of the time, you will be working on the business, doing admin, dealing with staff issues and paying bills. How much you can earn in a day is effectively capped.

CASE STUDY: A CLIENT LEARNS TO VALUE HERSELF

A client approached me, tired and overwhelmed and wondering how she was going to keep her business afloat. She told me she seemed to have no time to complete tasks, was running herself into the ground and struggling to work in the business, never mind on the business. Quality time with her family and friends was nonexistent.

I offered her ten mentoring sessions where we looked at her entire business model. Not only was she tied up in every part of her business, from admin to accounts, but she was also charging a low rate for her time. When we factored in the cost of the products she needed to service her clients, we discovered she was working for no money at all.

This entrepreneur did not love herself enough, so she didn't value her own time. She was late for every meeting she had with clients and was starting to lose them because of this. She was effectively sabotaging her own business by losing clients' trust.

We worked together to get to the root of the problem. After a while, she realised that most of her problems were based around fear. She was afraid to be seen, to put herself out there, and felt she didn't deserve to earn money. To her, money was about material things, about ego, which gave her an unhealthy connection with it.

We talked through all these issues and drew up a plan. She understood that she would go through a lot of healing in the process and was happy to do so. When we had completed our sessions, she was like a different person. She understood why she had such a dislike for money and now no longer charges on an hourly basis for her services, but on the value of the project she is working on. The money she earns, she spends on her children, self-care and personal and business development. Best of all, she is proud of how much she has changed and how far she has come.

Partnerships

When we meet someone, our gut instantly tells us whether we like them or not. We may feel a connection with a person because we believe our values are aligned or we have a similar mindset. When our energy connects, we are drawn to that person as if we have known each other for many years. Although we may not realise why, we want to know more about them on a deeper level.

In business, this connection is imperative if we want to have a partnership with an individual or company. We see how the person presents themselves and how they perform. If their actions match their words, we trust them because they are good at their profession and can deliver on their promise. Based on what we have seen so far, we feel they are a good fit for our company. They offer a solution to our problem.

Trust is the key to a successful partnership. This is the unspoken bond between two people in business. When we trust a business partner, we believe that when we communicate our vision for our goals to them, they will follow our desires to the highest standard. In return, we are happy to make payment for their services.

A business is a group of individuals with a clear vision and direction. As the business owner, we know where we want to take it and choose to work with likeminded individuals to achieve our goal. When we follow our gut, we can rest assured that we are making the right decisions at the right time and working with the right partners to move our business forward. We want someone to push us and open our mind to new ideas, but not to take us so far off our path that we move away from our core values.

When we go against our gut and make a decision based on what we think we should do, not what is right for us and our business, we may end up working with a business partner who is not in line with our vision. We give them our brief and they produce something which is completely different to our vision. In other words, they interpret their own ideas and don't listen to or even care about our vision.

Business partners like this tend only to want to make a quick buck and don't care how they get it. They are led by their ego rather than being led by their heart, so every business interaction is transactional. They hurt their fellow business owners but, more importantly, they hurt themselves by not working with integrity, as this shines through in their delivery. If they don't listen to and align with their clients' values and visions, those clients will retaliate with poor reviews and no repeat business, often without giving reasons for their decision. Once trust is broken, it cannot be repaired.

You may take a wrong path and decide to work with a business partner you later discover is not a good fit for you. The key is not to see this as a negative, but a part of your journey, an opportunity to learn. Make the decision to dissolve a partnership with someone who is not aligned with your values. Don't beat yourself up for the choices you've made; instead, learn from the challenges you've had to overcome. Like a chameleon, you'll then adapt to every situation you are faced with. Recognise the growth you've gained and be grateful for the experiences you've gone through to get there and the people who supported you in the difficult times. Realise how resilient you are becoming.

CASE STUDY: HOW TO BUILD TRUST

A client approached me recently. He'd had a difficult experience with his previous accountant which made him sceptical of me and he did not want to disclose much information. For most of the meeting, he held his cards close to his chest and remained cautious throughout.

I asked my standard list of questions to gather the information that I needed. I told him about my background and my accountancy journey and saw him slowly soften. When I showed him clearly that I was not judging him or treating him any differently to my other clients, he began to connect with me and open up slightly.

After a few months, he was a completely different person around me compared to our first meeting. I asked him what had changed. He explained to me that he had previously been working with one of the top five accountancy practices in the country and had felt intimidated by the offices and the questions the accountant asked him. Overall, he felt a bit out of his depth. He told me that I had immediately made him feel comfortable because I was interested in his business journey, and he would recommend me to his friends and business owners alike.

Opportunities

When we are open minded, we embrace opportunities and experiences that we would not otherwise have had access to. We see the world through a different lens. It has colour; it is exciting; it becomes an endless list of chances to learn more about ourselves. There are no limits to what we can achieve with an open mind.

When we embrace opportunities, we meet interesting individuals outside of our immediate circle. We strike up conversations with these people who introduce us to others in their network, who in turn introduce us to yet more influential people, and before long we are surrounded by support to take our business idea forward. We receive constructive feedback from these supporters to improve on every aspect of our life, including our personal brand, our business and the people we surround ourselves with. This allows our ideas to take shape rapidly.

When we seize the opportunities to gain momentum in our business, things fall into place with little planning or energy. Surrounded by likeminded people – our tribe – who love what we are doing and are delighted with our success, we are highly supported and know we are on the right path. We listen to our mentors and take the action steps they suggest. People are drawn towards our energy.

To embrace opportunities, we need to remain curious about life. We need to feel like a child who has received a new toy and cannot wait to play with it. With opportunities come ideas and an abundance of choices.

Sometimes we can get overwhelmed by which idea to run with first, so it is important to stay grounded. If we have too many ideas in our head, we must catch ourselves and make sure each idea is within the realms of reality. Our imagination is powerful, but when it comes up with ideas such as travelling to Mars to start a business there, we need to remind ourselves to be realistic. Although we want our goals to be big and scary and take us out of our comfort zone, we need to focus on what is doable and discard what is not.

When life feels good and everything is in balance, things may seem too easy. We can then sometimes worry that any day now, we are going to fail. We are living our best life while others are struggling around us. Why?

It's all about mindset. If they don't have the mindset to spot and embrace opportunities, there's nothing we can do to help them until they change that mindset. They may regard us as lucky because good things seem to happen to us so easily, but the reality is we took the opportunities that came our way and did the hard work. We shifted our thinking patterns.

Once we realise we have it within us to change our thinking, it empowers us. Life can happen for us rather than against us because we are in control of it, not the other way around. We carve out the life that we desire by opening ourselves up. We stop, take a breath and decide we are going to live a life that gives us gifts in return for our hard work.

Trust

When we decide to work in partnership with someone, it always needs to be based on trust. The trust may be small at the beginning, but it grows over time with each transaction or meeting.

When we are paying our hard-earned cash to a company or business partner, we want to ensure we get what we've paid for and our expectations are matched by the product or service that we receive. For this to happen, it's vitally important for us to explain in detail what those expectations are and ensure our gut tells us the business partner is the right fit for us. Do they share our vision and understand our business ethos? If we are not aligned, the outcome can be disastrous and neither party will want to work with the other in the future.

When two parties trust each other, the bond is strong. We can work together smoothly with clients and partners and achieve the desired outcome for all of us.

This is just as important to personal relationships as it is to a successful business relationship.

Communication is the key factor to having a strong bond of trust and ensuring both parties are singing from the same hymn sheet. It all comes back to the same thing: if all parties are aligned and heading towards the same goal, then they will move forward together with ease. For a business, this will be reflected in healthy profits.

As a business owner, you need to have not only your partners aligned, but also your employees. Define your vision clearly to all parties and, more importantly, stick to it. If you are chopping and changing every few months, your partners and staff become unsettled and lose trust in you. When they lose trust, they no longer feel safe in their role and are uneasy around you. They'll stop respecting you and their level of work reduces, or they'll look for other opportunities outside of your organisation and you end up losing your best people.

I'm sure you can recall a time when you lost trust in a company. You probably felt let down, maybe even hurt by the company, and you no longer believed in the authenticity of its long-term goal. You may have complained to the business owner, you may never have told them how their business's failure to keep your trust affected you; either way, it's pretty much impossible for the owner to rebuild the relationship.

Instead, you're likely to move away from them and work with another company that respects your trust and better suits your values.

What about companies with more than one owner? Each owner may have a different vision for the business, which can lead to a successful outcome, but it is imperative that they all stay in constant conversation and communicate their thoughts. There is no room for a power struggle or for one party to have their needs met more than the others.

Problems inevitably arise when one owner does what they believe to be best for them rather than the overall success of the business. They may break off from the main plan to suit their own needs while the other business owners are oblivious and continue working on the path they all agreed in the first place. The energy and focus directed towards the mutual goal becomes fractured and, in most cases, the business goal is never reached. The business then fails due to a lack of sales, so there's no money in the bank to pay the creditors. The supply chain stops and the business can no longer continue. The trust is broken between the owners and cannot be repaired.

CASE STUDY: TIME TO SAY GOODBYE

A few years ago, two owners of a private limited company made an appointment to see me. At the start of their business, their vision had been clear and aligned, but as time passed, the end goal became diluted as each owner had changed their vision without discussing it with the other. Somewhere along the way, the communication had broken down and the trust had depleted.

As their personalities were different, I could easily see why each one had different views on how the business should progress. They had lost sight of the end goal and were too focused on what the other was not doing. Instead, they needed to focus on their own actions and align them to drive the business forward. If this did not work, they would need to go their separate ways before there was a complete breakdown in communication.

Even though the two owners were emotionally attached to the business, it soon became clear to me that the best thing for them was to go their separate ways. They agreed this was the right decision both emotionally and financially, and within the next few months, they split the profits, wound up the company and closed the bank account. They have both moved forward with their lives and each runs a successful business in a completely different industry.

When you as a business owner meet a client for the first time, you need to build trust quickly to show them you are not only competent at what you do, but you respect their privacy. Never disclose other clients' details to them and keep examples of the work you have done for others anonymous, thereby showing both your competence and integrity at the same time. Build trust by connecting with clients on their level and understanding their needs. Show them by your actions when you solve their problem for them that you are the go-to expert.

Toolkit to success

Throughout the chapters of this book, we have gone through the elements a successful entrepreneur needs to put in place, but the key is to work with them simultaneously. That sounds more difficult than it is as we have already worked through the elements in advance. Once we have learned it, each element continues to run within our subconscious mind, which does all the hard work for us.

With the right elements in place and working away in our subconscious mind until they become second nature to us, when we come to take action towards our dream goal, we find that many barriers we previously worried about have vanished. We become more determined than ever because, with these barriers gone, we can see the big picture clearly in our mind and want to make major life changes to get there for ourselves and our family. With the resilience we have built, we can focus on projects for longer periods of time, working through each problem that arises with ease as it doesn't have the same negative impact on us as it did before. We do not take setbacks personally and feel equipped to deal with the next issue that comes our way.

Focused on the direction we are moving in, we gain momentum. We are more confident within ourselves and can make decisions faster, using our intuition as we now believe in its power. We also stick to our decisions rather than acting like a magpie and being attracted to anything new and shiny.

With this focus, the things we want come to fruition and materialise before our eyes in a short space of time. When we are achieving the small targets we set ourselves on the way to achieving our big goal, we feel a shift of energy within ourselves as we get excited about our life once again.

When we change our life for the better, all our relationships improve. We make more time for ourselves and our family by grouping similar activities together and completing them as a batch. As we gain more time, we can increase our self-care as we now believe that we are as important as everyone else around us and we cannot help others if our energy is depleted.

With more experience beneath our belt, we can become mentors and talk about what we have gone through to those who are following in our footsteps, saving them years of wrong turns and mistakes. Our experiences have given us immense, unique growth and we are grateful for each and every one of them, especially the more difficult ones as they have given us the most growth. We need to go through the pain to appreciate the growth.

The most successful people in this world don't necessarily come from rich families. Many tell a story of poverty or hardship that they were no longer prepared to accept. They refused to believe that this is the only way to live and chose to make major changes so their children wouldn't have to suffer as they did. They want to make a difference in the world and carve out a good life for themselves.

This quite simply is the key to entrepreneurial success. We may all have different goals and we certainly all have a unique story, but using this toolkit for success, we will succeed.

EXERCISE: LET IT GO

It's not just emotional baggage that can weigh us down. Material possessions can also stop us moving forwards and achieving our goals – you're probably familiar with the idea that if you have an untidy house, office or car, you will have an untidy mind.

For this exercise, identify an area where you are holding onto things that are no longer serving you. This could be clothes that no longer fit but which you keep because they remind you of your youth; your child's old baby toys, which you have held onto as a keepsake; or clutter on your desk that you are afraid to throw away 'in case I need it one day'.

Be honest with yourself and take the opportunity to declutter. Throw away anything that is no longer useful and donate anything with life left in it to a charity shop or offer it to a neighbour or friend.

Be ruthless: getting rid of those things that no longer serve you will free mental and physical space for newer, fresher things that will add real value to your life.

Summary

In this chapter, we have looked at what makes a successful entrepreneur different to other people. We've seen how keeping an open mind is essential to spotting opportunities for growth. We've learned how to value ourselves and our products and services so we can charge what our expertise is worth and make sure we never again work for free. We've recognised how communication of clear boundaries and setting a goal that aligns with everyone's values builds trust and respect with business partners, employees and clients alike. Our values are then felt throughout the business.

We've also seen what can happen when trust breaks down. Sometimes as entrepreneurs, we must accept that a business relationship was never going to work for any party, learn from the experience and move on. The lessons we take with us will stand us in good stead to follow our hearts and make a success of a new venture.

Finally, we brought together everything we have learned in this book into a toolkit for entrepreneurial success.

7
Dream

In this chapter, we will see how our dream, our vision, is converting into reality through the goals we have chosen. Now is the time to process our emotions and appreciate everything we have worked for. Having done the inner work, we are reaping the rewards, and the feelings and experiences we have gone through will stay with us forever, but we must remain grateful for all these things because they will turn our lives around and give us so much joy.

Let's now have a look at how our dream is likely to manifest itself and what we can do to make sure it continues to become reality.

Financial freedom

This can mean different things to different people. Maybe you see yourself as financially free if you have paid off your mortgage. Maybe your children have left home and you no longer have dependents to pay for. It could mean that you have enough surplus cash to travel the world and never work another day in your life, doing what you want when you want to.

To me, being financially free means our decisions are not ruled by the amount of money we have in our bank account. It allows us to be independent, giving us more options and choices to work only when we want. We have time to dedicate to our health, family, friends and hobbies. We can now give back in the form of mentoring or volunteering.

Whatever financial freedom means to you, it has the desired outcome: every penny you spend from now on will be pleasurable rather than laden with guilt and worry that you can't really afford it. With financial freedom, you can spoil yourself, donate to charity or improve your self-image. You become quietly abundant within yourself and have a lot to give to others. A word of warning, though: before achieving financial freedom, you have to deal with any negative relationship you may have with money.

Have you ever wondered why some lottery winners lose all their money within a year of gaining it? The reason this happens is because they often do not feel worthy or deserving of being materially rich. They buy as many items as they can – cars, boats, lavish holidays – to get rid of the money as fast as possible. Deep down, they may believe money is evil and they are not equipped to handle a large amount of it.

When you move through the steps to success outlined in the SQUARED model, you earn money slowly and consistently. This affords you the opportunity to heal any negative emotional connection you may have with money, giving you the right mindset to spend what you have wisely and earn more.

There are many ways to make money as an entrepreneur. We can even be making money in our sleep, which is what many of us strive for; there are plenty of money-making activities that are separate from our main day-to-day income. Perhaps we have shares in a company or have purchased an entire company outright. This can grow our returns exponentially. Trading on the stock exchange can be extremely profitable because each market opens at a different time throughout the day, so it's a twenty-four-hour activity. This allows us to complete our daily trading at a time that suits us. By putting in the effort to learn this skill, we can become highly successful on the stock market.

We may make passive income from property for which we receive monthly rent with few costs or outgoings. Property development can seem risky, but with the right strategy and mentor to take you through the process, the rewards are high and offset the risk when we're successful.

Investing our money in long-term bonds or ISAs can give us a higher return than our standard high-street bank, but our money is locked away for many years and we cannot access it on demand. Multilevel marketing – the practice of earning commission by selling something on behalf of a company – can make us money while we sleep. We can be involved as little or as much as we choose, but our level of input has a direct impact on our level of success. Although we can earn lots of money in this way, I recommend caution. Some multilevel marketing practices are not as ethical as they may at first appear to be.

CASE STUDY: HOW A CLIENT GAINED FINANCIAL FREEDOM

A client had worked for many years, growing their business to a point where it was making six figures per annum. They had also invested well in property and had passive rental income from that.

My client had a substantial mortgage and was working hard to repay this in full so that they owned their properties outright, but they suddenly became ill and weren't able to claim on their life insurance policy. They were still receiving monthly rental income from their property portfolio, though.

This client decided to sell their company to a bigger competitor within the same industry and received a large payout in return. They now own all their investment properties outright so they have no debt, and they make surplus cash from the rental payments, so they have the option never to work again and can travel the world if they so wish. They are free of all financial claims on them and delight in the fact that they have no ties or stress.

Goals

Without a goal or purpose to focus our energy towards, we will have no direction to move in. We may then drift through life, wavering in this direction or that like a paper bag in the wind with no idea where we are going or where we will end up. This is not the way to feel good within ourselves.

We may dream up a few ideas that we believe to be goals, but with no emotional attachment to them, we're likely to give up within a few weeks when they haven't taken off. Get-rich-quick schemes suddenly have appeal, but these are pretty much guaranteed to fail. We want to aim to get rich both materially and personally, and there's no quick way to do that. Without clear direction and a goal we believe in to focus our energy towards, we may even feel depressed. There must be more to life than this.

Rest assured, there is. The best thing to do is work with a mentor to get you out of any rut you may be in. When I work with my clients, the first thing we do is to set their goals in alignment with their true values and plan how they can achieve those goals.

Look at where you are in your life and where you want to be in twelve months. Home in on every section of your life, scrutinising each part like you are seeing it through a microscope, and decide what you want to change. A mentor will guide you through each stage and help make sure it takes you to where you want to be – to your dream. You can then plan the changes you wish to make.

List all the changes you want to see in each aspect of your life and break them down into manageable tasks that you can work through each day. Then take action on five tasks a day. These bite-sized pieces stop you from becoming overwhelmed by the enormity of the goal while you work steadily towards it. Within a few short weeks or months, you will be halfway there.

Your mentor will act as your accountability partner when you feel lost, feel like giving up or lose your focus, guiding you through each stage until you reach your goal. Even when you know the steps you need to take to achieve your goal, you may still procrastinate or tell yourself that you will do it tomorrow. The knowing-doing gap is real.

You need to roll up your sleeves and do the hard work. Get stuck in there and make decisions and act, fast. Remember the five-second rule? You want to start on today's action steps before your brain kicks in to tell you that you'd far rather be doing something else. Here is where a mentor can be worth their weight in gold to keep you accountable during the difficult times when you want to give up.

When you are moving through the fear barrier, it is often not a pretty sight. You are under stress, stretched to your maximum and feeling like you want to give up. The people who love you will want to make life easy for you and are likely to suggest you stop as they don't want you to struggle any more. It is often much easier to go back to where you were rather than grow, but you will ultimately regret this decision. Listen to your gut and your mentor and fulfil your purpose in life, your raison d'être.

When you choose a mentor to hold you accountable, it makes moving towards your goal much simpler. Your mentor is not emotionally attached to you or your goal; their role is to listen to your wants and desires and match them to your actions. Think of a mentor as a personal trainer in life, helping you to mark off and celebrate each milestone you pass. It is important to stop and reflect on how far you have come and reward yourself for the journey you have travelled so far. This gives you momentum for working on the next stage of your goal.

COMFORT ZONE	FEAR ZONE	LEARNING ZONE	GROWTH ZONE
Feel safe and in control	Affected by others' opinions	Deal with challenges and problems	Find purpose
	Find excuses	Acquire new skills	Live dreams
	Lack self-confidence	Extend the comfort zone	Set new goals
			Realise aspirations

There is a great article on the *Positive Psychology* website that shows the journey we take when we leave our comfort zone.[15] When we start our growth journey, we may feel uncomfortable as we stretch. We move from our comfort zone through the fear barrier to the learning zone, which is the sweet spot. This is where we make big changes. Our thoughts and feelings become aligned and our dreams take shape. Finally, we enter the growth zone, which is where all our hard work becomes a reality and our ideas come to fruition.

Vision

Our vision is an ensemble of all our goals combined. The vision of achieving our dream and living a life fulfilled may change many times and come to us in many ways. Some people visit psychics or mediums for guidance; some use tarot cards; some use meditation, which simply involves being at peace with our thoughts. We can meditate while walking in a beautiful place, such as in a forest or by the sea, noticing our surroundings, our thoughts and our feelings.

We can get a lot of clarity when we meditate. It quietens the brain and grounds us so we can feel what our gut is telling us. Many of us spend all day in our heads and are disconnected from our intuition. When

---

15 O Page, 'How to leave your comfort zone and enter your growth zone', *Positive Psychology* (2022), https://positivepsychology.com/comfort-zone, accessed 18 May 2022

we are in tune with what our gut is telling us, we pick up on areas of pain or stress that we need to work on releasing. If we are not aware of this pain, it goes untreated for years and can develop into something more serious.

Every physical pain can be traced back to an emotional state. When we're aware of our emotional pain points, we can heal them with affirmations to remove the stuck energy from our body. This method was developed by Louise Hay during the 1970s when she cured herself of cancer.[16] In the same way as Louise used affirmations to heal her, we can use them when striving for our goals.

All the answers we need are within us and meditation shows us our higher selves in the form of images from our subconscious mind. We believe in things more readily when we see them visually, so these images help us to cement our true goals. Meditation stops us from having irrational fears and allows us to become the best versions of ourselves.

Repeat

We now know how to create an idea, form it into a goal that is aligned with our values, believe in the process and take the action steps to make it reality, but

---

16 L Hay, 'About Louise' (no date), www.louisehay.com/about, accessed 5 April 2022

what happens when we have succeeded in achieving our goal? We then repeat the process multiple times over multiple businesses, compounding our learning and constantly refining our processes until we achieve the maximum outcome possible: our vision.

Whatever type of business you start, you cannot take your eye of the ball and lose sight of your vision. Never make the mistake of starting a second or third business before the first one is completely stable, with strong foundations in place. If you do not have the right staff, software or systems in place, the result will be poor teamwork leading to inefficiencies which cause the company to haemorrhage money.

When you have good systems in place in your first business, it will get to the point where it almost runs itself. You'll have few day-to-day activities to carry out, allowing you time to overview your company results and work towards creating your next business.

Many entrepreneurs start their second business in the same industry using the same business model as their first. They have tried and tested the processes in the first business and know they work effectively; the internal controls are strong and the inefficiencies are minimal. This means they don't have to put much work into growing the second business to the same level as the first. They have learned from their experiences and don't make the same mistakes, so they reach their goal quickly as they eliminate all the processes that did not work first time around.

The problem with doing this is that while we can make a lot of money quickly, we do not learn much from the subsequent project and as a result, we stall our growth. We feel less and less rewarded for our hard work and may eventually lose interest in all our businesses.

What happens when we as business owners decide to start a second business in a different industry, one that is new to us? Let's say we receive an opportunity in a field that we know nothing about. We can see the potential of the project; our heart is telling us that it is a brilliant opportunity, but our head is telling us to seek out more information. This is exactly what we do.

We engage a mentor to help us cost the project and see the figures in black and white. They back up what our heart is telling us: that the project is financially viable, so we decide to move forward with it. We are now in growth mode as we move through the steps of the project, learning about the industry as we go. We listen to our mentor and follow their guidance at each point, and before we know it, we're halfway through the project and have learned so much. Buzzing with excitement at how far we have come, we cannot wait to take the business to the next level.

We can do this multiple times with similar projects in different fields; the key is to wait until one project is at least three-quarters finished before we start the next one. This stops us from becoming overwhelmed and juggling too many things at one time, which can make us feel that we do not know where to go next, so we stop altogether. With the right support and advice from likeminded people who only want us to succeed, we can achieve anything we put our mind to.

EXERCISE: WHAT WE TELL OURSELVES MATTERS

Affirmations are positive statements that can help you shift your mindset and change the way your body and brain deal with challenges. Follow these steps to write and use affirmations to overcome difficulties and empower you to take control of your life:

- First, identify an area of your life that you want to improve.
- Look at this area and decide what you don't like about it currently – what do you wish to change and why do you want to change it?
- Write a short sentence that is the opposite of your current belief. It should be in the present tense and use only positive words. For example, if you believe that you are powerless and stuck in a situation, you could write, 'I have the power to change my life.'
- Say the sentence out loud to yourself, feeling each word as you say it.
- Repeat the affirmation regularly until you feel a shift take place within yourself and notice that you now feel differently about this issue.

Once you notice this shift, you have changed your mindset, healed yourself from within. You can return the affirmation as often as you need to.

Summary

In this chapter, we brought together everything that we have worked on throughout the book, from setting our goal to seeing which parts of our life are causing us to be stuck to what we need to do to make the essential changes, keeping our focus on our vision and dream at all stages, especially the difficult ones. We remember to appreciate what we have and reward ourselves for our successes when we make some changes.

With focus on our dream, our goal and vision, and the help of a mentor, we can quieten the negative self-talk in our head, deal with any poor relationship we may have with money and gain an understanding of what financial freedom means to us. In this chapter, we learned some ways to achieve financial freedom, which allows us to made strides towards our goal and set ourselves new bigger goals.

We feel the growth within us from the experiences and issues we deal with along the way to each goal. As we move away from negative people and surround ourselves with support, we see our vision materialise bit by bit. With this growth comes the knowledge and confidence to repeat what we have learned by setting a new goal that is bigger and scarier than the previous one and starting a business in an entirely different sector, thereby growing even more.

Conclusion

In this book, we have travelled through many stages of growth to achieve our end goal, our dream. At the start, we may have been somewhat lost, with little or no direction or clarity on what we wanted in life. We didn't know ourselves as we had not studied ourselves and were unaware of our true likes and dislikes. This prevented us from setting boundaries for ourselves and others, including clients, which made the people around us unsure about us and maybe even mistrust us.

As we learn more about ourselves, we can strengthen those boundaries and clearly define our vision, goals and values to everyone. Our values can then shine through in everything we do, drawing likeminded people, including our ideal clients, towards us with little or no effort on our part. When we trust in ourselves, others trust in us too. This raises our confidence and self-esteem.

At this point, we have removed old habits that no longer serve us and have the strength within us to make bigger and better decisions for ourselves and our families. Once we break the learned behaviour of our past, we open up a whole host of new ideas that we can choose to accept or reject.

When we scrutinise ourselves and strip back the beliefs we have held up until now in our life – beliefs often projected on to us by others when we were children – we may feel vulnerable. This is understandable: we are at the starting point of the journey to becoming a new person. When we learn about our authentic self, we have nothing to hide. We become more confident than we have ever been and project this feeling on to others, energising them and giving them a burst of positivity so they too want to create and develop ideas, goals and dreams.

This positivity can be short lived, though. Until others do the hard internal work required to drive a goal from seed to reality for themselves, all we have done is motivate them. We need to guide them to change their old patterns, just like we did, and turn into a resilient, patient go getter with a mentor and accountability to support them through the growing pains.

CONCLUSION

As a mentor myself, I support entrepreneurs through this journey as I have walked it many times. I understand the pain they are currently in and help them to decide if they want to continue as they are or make the hard decision to move towards their goal and choose a better life.

The true benefit of a goal is not what we arrive at, but the journey we travel to get there; that's where the growth happens. We experience many emotions as we grow and can often doubt ourselves, losing hope, passion and sight of why we started in the first place. Sometimes, we don't have a dream at all or have too many to know which one we feel most passionate about. A mentor will help guide us through the process, highlighting the pros and cons of each goal until we come to a decision that resonates with our intuition. This is where the excitement starts, when we find what we really care about and want to see it through to the end.

Watching my clients become excited and achieve their dreams brings me such joy. I understand that they have the tools they need to achieve their heart's desire within them and all I am doing is bringing these to the surface.

If you would like to work with a mentor towards a goal in either your professional or personal life, I am offering anyone with a copy of this book a free one-hour one-to-one goalsetting session. In this hour, we will look at your current position, see where you want to be in twelve months and reverse engineer the steps required to get you there. You will take away tips to take action towards your goal and make immediate changes to your life. If you are interested, please visit the 'Author' section at the end of the book for my contact details.

However you choose to move forward with your life, I urge you to make the decision today to become the best version of yourself. With the advice in this book and a mentor by your side, you'll have everything you need to unlock the skills that are inherent within you. You've got this!

Acknowledgements

I owe much to my high-performance mentor, Kim Calvert. Meeting Kim made a huge difference to my life. She taught me that I should think big, and then all the small stuff would naturally dissolve. She supported me through the massive upheavals which have changed my life in the best way.

I want to thank my lovely beta readers, who took the time to read my book and give me feedback on the content. Special thanks go to Linda Carmichael, Alison Matthews, Ann Rimmer and Miriam Van Heusden.

I would like to thank Karen Hillis, who took the time to write my fantastic foreword, and Linda Hyde for the subtitle.

I would also like to give a special thanks to my parents, Olive and Peter Grant, who give me strength and resilience and have supported me throughout my life. To them, I am forever grateful.

I have dedicated my book to my amazing children, and I would also like to acknowledge them here for supporting me to achieve my goals.

The Author

Melanie Coey gained a degree in applied mathematics at Queen's University, Belfast, then completed a professional accountancy qualification with the Institute of Financial Accountants. After working for manufacturing and engineering companies for twenty years at financial controller level, she started her own business and is now director of M Squared Accountancy Ltd, a successful cloud-based accountancy practice.

Using the most up-to-date software, Melanie works in conjunction with mortgage and pension advisors and human-resources specialists to offer a full suite of financial services, including self-assessment tax returns, accounts for sole trader and limited companies, VAT returns, payroll bureau and a full business mentoring service.

- 🌐 https://msquaredaccountancy.co.uk
- ❙ www.facebook.com/msquaredaccountancy
- ❙ www.linkedin.com/in/melanie-coey-accountant-428a30100
- ❙ @MSquaredAccount
- ❙ @m_squared_accountancy_ltd